MAGRUDER'S

Primary Source and Reading Guide

American Government

INTERACTIVE

SAVVAS

LEARNING COMPANY

ISBN-13: 978-1-418-39166-9
ISBN-10:   1-418-39166-2

2 22

Topic 1 Foundations of Government and Citizenship

Topic 2 The Beginnings of American Government

Topic 3 The Constitution

Topic 4 The Legislative Branch

Topic 5 The Executive Branch: The Presidency and Vice Presidency

Topic 6 The Executive Branch at Work

CLOSE READING

PRIMARY SOURCES

Topic 7 The Judicial Branch

CLOSE READING

PRIMARY SOURCES

Topic 8 Protecting Civil Liberties

Topic 9 Citizenship and Civil Rights

Topic 10 Government by the People

Topic 11 Elections

Topic 12 Government and the Economy

Topic 13 State and Local Government

Topic 14 Comparative Political Systems

CLOSE READING

PRIMARY SOURCES

Lesson 1 Principles of Government

CLOSE READING

Government—We the People

1. **Identify Supporting Details** As you read "Government—We the People," fill out this three-circle Venn diagram to show how the three basic powers possessed by all governments combine to make up a government. For each power, insert an example.

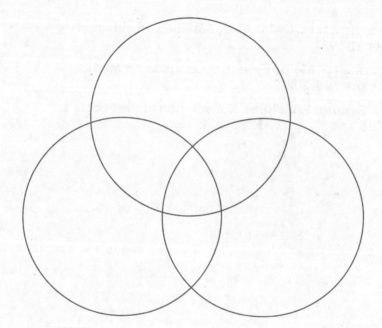

2. **Compare and Contrast** How is a government conducted under a dictatorship? How is a dictatorship different from a democracy?

The State

3. **Describe** What is the difference between a state and a nation?

4. **Identify Cause and Effect** Read the discussion of Thomas Hobbes's ideas about why states need government. Why did Thomas Hobbes consider government necessary? Use the text to support your answer.

How States Arose

5. **Cite Evidence** Read the paragraphs about the social contract theory. Cite evidence from the Declaration of Independence that shows that the signers believed in this theory.

6. **Draw Conclusions** Review the section of text that discusses the historical development of governments and describes the four theories of the origin of the state. Which two theories do you think a dictator might claim as justification for taking power? Why?

What Government Does

7. **Determine Central Ideas** Why is a written constitution important for governing a state?

8. **Draw Inferences** How might widespread access to education promote the general welfare?

Lesson 2 Types of Government

CLOSE READING

Classifying Governments

1. **Draw Inferences** Why is geographical distribution of power important in the United States?

2. **Draw Conclusions** Why is the relationship between the executive and legislative branches a useful way to classify governments?

Who Can Participate?

3. **Make Comparisons** How does the U.S. constitutional republic compare to authoritarian forms of government?

4. **Contrast** What characteristics does a theocracy have that are missing in the U.S. constitutional republic form of government? Explain.

Geographic Distribution of Power

5. **Synthesize** Analyze the advantages and disadvantages of the federal, confederate, and unitary systems of government. Include at least two advantages and two disadvantages of each system in the table below.

System of Government	Advantages	Disadvantages
Federal		
Unitary		
Confederate		

6. **Cite Evidence** While there are three ways to classify government (the number of persons who can participate, where power resides, and the relationship between the executive and legislative branches), many people find it most useful to classify governments by the number of people who can participate in the government. Why do you think this is so? Cite evidence from the text to support your answer.

Legislative and Executive Branches

7. **Analyze** Analyze the advantages and disadvantages of parliamentary systems of government.

Lesson 3 Origins of the Modern Democratic State

CLOSE READING

Building on the Past

1. **Compare and Contrast** How were the governments of ancient Athens and the Roman Republic similar? How were they different?

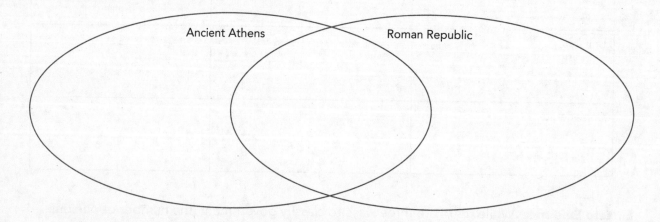

Ancient Athens   Roman Republic

2. **Identify Supporting Details** What aspects of government did the Roman Republic share with a true democracy?

Nations and Kings

3. **Identify Cause and Effect** What impact did the Black Plague have on the rise of mercantilism?

4. **Determine Meaning of Words** What do you think the term *absolute monarchy* means? What impact did absolute monarchy have on monarchs' ability to establish governments?

Power, Authority, and Legitimacy

5. **Summarize** What approaches are used by rulers to gain legitimacy?

European Colonialism

6. **Determine Central Ideas** What was the ultimate goal that drove monarchs to colonize and to establish international trade routes?

Power Comes from the People

7. **Paraphrase** In your own words, describe the philosophies of the Baron de Montesquieu and John Locke.

8. **Explain an Argument** Explain Blackstone's concept of common law.

Lesson 4 The Basics of Democracy

CLOSE READING

Foundations of Democracy

1. **Summarize** Use the chart to list the five basic notions of democracy. Then explain what each means to a U.S. citizen.

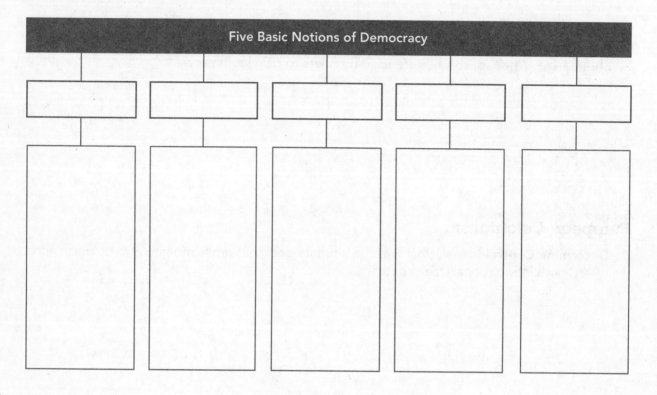

Five Basic Notions of Democracy

2. **Paraphrase** Explain the concept of *majority rule* in your own words.

3. **Compare and Contrast** Compare and contrast the following two quotations from the text:

   "The right to swing my fist ends where the other man's nose begins."

   —*Justice Oliver Wendell Holmes*

   "The rights of every man are diminished when the rights of one man are threatened."

   —*John F. Kennedy*

Responsibilities, Duties, and Obligations of Citizenship

4. Determine Central Ideas Theodore Roosevelt said: "The first requisite of a good citizen in our republic is that he should be able and willing to pull his weight." What does this mean to a U.S. citizen?

Democracy and the Free Enterprise System

5. Use Visual Information Look at the art that illustrates the concept of capitalism and the free enterprise system. The second pillar is labeled *Individual Initiative*. Considering that the word *initiative* means "the energy and desire that is needed to do something," what do you think *individual initiative* means? According to the drawing, how does it relate to capitalism?

6. Draw Conclusions What is government's role in the free enterprise system?

PRIMARY SOURCE

Speech: Inaugural Address, President Barack Obama, January 21, 2013

The inauguration of the President of the United States, a time-honored tradition that dates back to 1789, is a ceremony to mark the commencement of a new four-year term of the President. On January 21, 2013, Barack Obama took his presidential oath of office for a second term. In his inaugural address, President Obama alludes to the creation of this nation as a republic. He notes that, in forming this republic, the American people rejected the long-standing traditions of tyrannical rule and unaccountable leadership.

Vice President Biden, Mr. Chief Justice, members of the United States Congress, distinguished guests, and fellow citizens:

Each time we gather to inaugurate a President we bear witness to the enduring strength of our Constitution. We affirm the promise of our democracy. We recall that what binds this nation together is not the colors of our skin or the tenets of our faith or the origins of our names. What makes us exceptional—what makes us American—is our allegiance to an idea articulated in a declaration made more than two centuries ago: 'We hold these truths to be self-evident, that all men are created equal; that they are endowed by their Creator with certain unalienable rights; that among these are life, liberty, and the pursuit of happiness.'

Today we continue a never-ending journey to bridge the meaning of those words with the realities of our time. For history tells us that while these truths may be self-evident, they've never been self-executing; that while freedom is a gift from God, it must be secured by His people here on Earth. (*Applause.*) The patriots of 1776 did not fight to replace the tyranny of a king with the privileges of a few or the rule of a mob. They gave to us a republic, a government of, and by, and for the people, entrusting each generation to keep safe our founding creed.

1. Based on President Obama's speech and your existing knowledge of American government, what characteristics protect a republic from both the "tyranny of a king" and "the rule of a mob"?

2. What does President Obama mean when he says "while these truths may be self-evident, they've never been self-executing"?

Speech: "The Spirit of Liberty," Judge Learned Hand, presented on "I Am an American Day" (now Citizenship Day), 1944

On May 21, 1944, Judge Learned Hand addressed a crowd of 1.5 million who attended a ceremony in Central Park in New York City. About 150,000 of those in attendance were becoming American citizens. In his address, he notes how all American citizens share a common devotion to liberty. Contrary to the common misconception of liberty, Judge Learned Hand emphasizes that liberty is not "the unbridled will . . . to do as one likes." Instead, it is a collective spirit of understanding and mutual respect and a commitment to preserving this belief.

We have gathered here to affirm a faith, a faith in a common purpose, a common conviction, a common devotion. Some of us have chosen America as the land of our adoption; the rest have come from those who did the same. For this reason we have some right to consider ourselves a picked group, a group of those who had the courage to break from the past and brave the dangers and the loneliness of a strange land. What was the object that nerved us, or those who went before us, to this choice? We sought liberty— freedom from oppression, freedom from want, freedom to be ourselves. . . . What do we mean when we say that first of all we seek liberty? . . . It is not the ruthless, the unbridled will; it is not freedom to do as one likes. That is the denial of liberty, and leads straight to its overthrow. A society in which men recognize no check upon their freedom soon becomes a society where freedom is the possession of only a savage few. . . .

. . . [T]he spirit of liberty is the spirit which seeks to understand the minds of other men and women; the spirit of liberty is the spirit which weighs their interest alongside its own without bias.

1. How does Judge Learned Hand's definition of liberty relate to the American concept of democracy?

2. In his speech, Judge Learned Hand emphasizes that liberty is not the same as unchecked freedom. Elaborate on why he believes this to be true.

Supreme Court Case:
Buchanan v. Warley, 1917

Charles H. Buchanan was a white individual who sold a house to William Warley, a Black individual in Louisville, Kentucky. However, Louisville had an ordinance that prohibited Black citizens from living on a block where the majority of residents were white. In a unanimous decision, the Court ruled that this ordinance was unconstitutional because it violated the Due Process Clause of the 14th Amendment, which prohibits the arbitrary deprivation of life, liberty, or property, considered foundational rights of all American citizens.

Majority Opinion of the Court, Justice William R. Day

This ordinance prevents the occupancy of a lot in the City of Louisville by a person of color in a block where the greater number of residences are occupied by white persons; where such a majority exists, colored persons are excluded. This interdiction [exclusion] is based wholly upon color—simply that and nothing more. . . .

This drastic measure is sought to be justified under the authority of the State in the exercise of the police power. It is said such legislation tends to promote the public peace by preventing racial conflicts. . . .

The authority of the State to pass laws in the exercise of the police power, having for their object the promotion of the public health, safety, and welfare . . . has been affirmed in numerous and recent decisions of this court. . . . But it is equally well established that the police power, broad as it is, cannot justify the passage of a law or ordinance which runs counter to the limitations of the Federal Constitution. . . .

The Federal Constitution and laws passed within its authority are, by the express terms of that instrument, made the supreme law of the land. The Fourteenth Amendment protects life, liberty, and property from invasion by the States without due process of law. . . .

It was designed to assure to the colored race the enjoyment of all the civil rights that, under the law, are enjoyed by white persons, and to give to that race the protection of the general government in that enjoyment. . . . It not only gave citizenship and the privileges of citizenship to persons of color, but it denied to any State the power to withhold from them the equal protection of the laws, and authorized Congress to enforce its provisions by appropriate legislation.

1. How does this unanimous court ruling stay true to the ideals of American democracy?

2. According to the text, what role does Congress play in securing equal rights?

Lesson 1 Origins of American Political Ideals

CLOSE READING

Origins of American Constitutional Government

1. **Determine Central Ideas** What were three basic concepts of government that the English brought with them to North America? How did these concepts influence constitutional government in America?

Influential Documents and Ideas

2. **Compare and Contrast** How are the Petition of Right and the English Bill of Rights similar? How are they different? Cite examples from the text to support your answer.

3. **Summarize** How are the notions of ordered, limited, and representative government reflected in the three landmark documents? Cite examples from each document.

Three Types of Colonies

4. **Identify Supporting Details** As you read "Three Types of Colonies," use this graphic organizer to record characteristics of each type of colony.

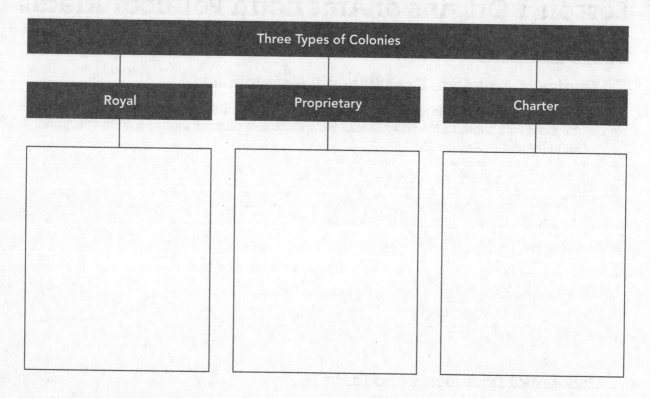

5. **Identify Cause and Effect** In what ways do you think the "stern hand" of the royal governors affected colonists' feelings toward the Crown?

6. **Use Visual Information** Look at the image of the "Charter Oak Tree," and read the caption that accompanies it. What does this information suggest about the feelings of the colonists in the time leading up to the Revolution?

7. **Summarize** How was the system of government different in the charter colonies than in the royal colonies? How did these differences impact the future of these colonies? Use supporting details from the text to support your answer.

Lesson 2 Independence

CLOSE READING

British Colonial Policies

1. **Analyze Interactions** Each colonial legislature operated fairly independently from England. Explain one way that these legislatures could exercise control over their royal governors.

Growing Colonial Unity

2. **Identify Cause and Effect** Think about why the colonies cooperated with each other. List one reason why each of the following was formed or took place.

New England Confederation	Albany meeting	Stamp Act Congress	Committees of Correspondence

The First Continental Congress

3. **Draw Conclusions** Why did the First Continental Congress send a Declaration of Rights to King George III instead of declaring war against England?

The Second Continental Congress

4. **Determine Central Ideas** List five responsibilities of the Second Continental Congress as the acting government of the colonies.

5. **Compare and Contrast** Think about the work undertaken by the Second Continental Congress. Name one way that it differed from the work of the First Continental Congress.

The Declaration of Independence

6. **Determine Meaning** Look at the text of the Declaration of Independence. According to this document, why are governments created?

7. **Determine Central Ideas** What made the political system described in the Declaration of Independence groundbreaking?

The First State Constitutions

8. **Integrate Information from Diverse Sources** What features of the first State constitutions were similar to ideas expressed in the Declaration of Independence?

Lesson 3 First Steps

CLOSE READING

The Articles of Confederation

1. **Summarize** Summarize the key debates that delayed approval of the Articles of Confederation and why these issues were important to the colonists.

2. **Cite Evidence** What evidence can you find in the text to support the idea that the Articles of Confederation sought to protect the independence of the States rather than to create a strong central government?

3. **Determine Central Ideas** In what ways did the States agree to support the Articles of Confederation? Why did Congress depend on this support in order to be effective?

A Time of Troubles, the 1780s

4. **Identify Cause and Effect** As you read "A Time of Troubles, the 1780s," use this graphic organizer to record the actions the States were able to take as a result of the weaknesses of the Articles.

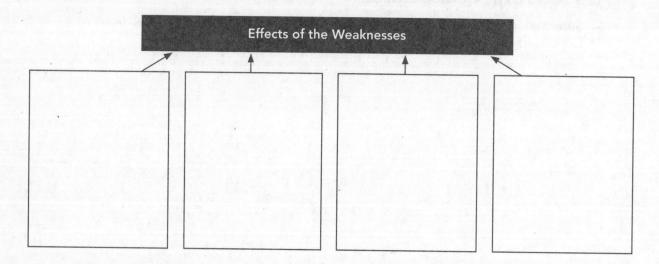

5. **Identify Cause and Effect** Explain how features of the Articles of Confederation led to the currency disaster that occurred following the Revolutionary War.

A Demand for Stronger Government

6. **Draw Conclusions** Which group led the movement toward a stronger government? What did they do and why? Use evidence from the text to support your answer.

7. **Analyze Interactions Among Events** In what way did the meetings at Mount Vernon in 1785, Annapolis in 1786, and Philadelphia in 1787 lead to the writing of the U.S. Constitution?

Lesson 4 Creating and Ratifying the Constitution

CLOSE READING

The Framers Meet

1. **Interpret** The delegates who attended the Philadelphia Convention, and who came to be known as the *Framers of the Constitution*, included many outstanding individuals. Yet, Patrick Henry remarked that he "smelt a rat" and refused to attend the Convention. To what would you attribute his comment?

The Delegates Adopt Rules of Procedure

2. **Determine Central Ideas** What was the proposed reason for holding the Constitutional Convention? How did that idea change based on the resolution by Edmund Randolph from Virginia?

Two Plans of Government

3. **Draw Inferences** Read the second paragraph of "The Virginia Plan." In the plan, Virginia suggested that one way to determine representation would be based on financial contributions from each State. What does this fact tell you about Virginia's economy and population relative to the other colonies?

4. **Compare and Contrast** Look at the chart in this text showing the features of the New Jersey Plan. In what way was the legislature created under this plan similar to the one that existed under the Articles of Confederation? Use a Venn diagram to compare the two plans.

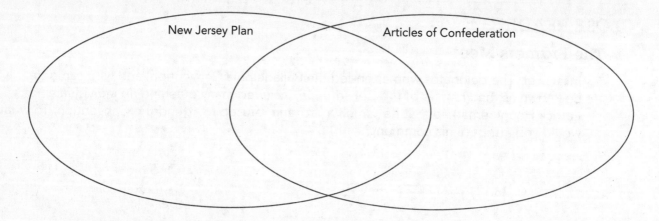

New Jersey Plan   Articles of Confederation

Debates and Compromises

5. **Support Ideas with Examples** Benjamin Franklin said that the convention spent much of its time "sawing boards to make them fit." Give three examples of decisions made during the Convention that support Franklin's comment.

6. **Integrate Information** Read the quotation below.

"... when you assemble a number of men to have the advantage of their joint wisdom, you inevitably assemble with those men, all their prejudices, their passions, their errors of opinion, their local interests, and their selfish views."

—*Benjamin Franklin*

Now recall that the Articles of Confederation had created a structure that more closely resembled an alliance of independent states than a united nation. What relationship can you find between that fact and Franklin's words?

The Fight for Ratification

7. **Identify Key Steps in a Process** Describe the process by which the U.S. Constitution was adopted.

PRIMARY SOURCE

Documents: Preamble to the Nigerian Constitution of 1999, Preamble to the U.S. Constitution

From the time it was written, the United States Constitution became an inspiration as well as a model for nations around the world. The first influences may be seen in the 1791 French Constitution. Later, its effects can be seen in the development of Latin American federalism, the reorganization of West Germany and Japan after World War II, and more recently, in the structure and language of new or revised constitutions in Middle Eastern and African nations.

In 1999, Nigeria discarded the parliamentary system it had inherited from Britain and adopted a new constitution that created a presidential government.

Preamble to the Nigerian Constitution of 1999

We the people of the Federal Republic of Nigeria
Having firmly and solemnly resolved:
TO LIVE in unity and harmony as one indivisible and indissoluble sovereign nation under God, dedicated to the promotion of inter-African solidarity, world peace, international co-operation and understanding
AND TO PROVIDE for a Constitution for the purpose of promoting the good government and welfare of all persons in our country, on the principles of freedom, equality and justice, and for the purpose of consolidating the unity of our people
DO HEREBY make, enact and give to ourselves the following Constitution:

Preamble to the United States Constitution

We the People of the United States, in Order to form a more perfect Union, establish Justice, insure domestic Tranquility, provide for the common defense, promote the general Welfare, and secure the Blessings of Liberty to ourselves and our Posterity, do ordain and establish this Constitution for the United States of America.

1. Identify similar phrases or words used in both preambles.

2. Why do you think the U.S. Constitution has had such an influence around the world and for so long?

Supreme Court Case:
United States v. *Curtiss-Wright Export Corporation*, 1936

In 1936, fighting broke out between Bolivia and Paraguay. The U.S. Congress passed a joint resolution giving the President the power to prohibit the sale of arms to either country. The President then issued an Executive Order establishing an embargo. Curtiss-Wright Export Corporation was later indicted for violating the embargo by selling munitions to Bolivia. Its defense was that Congress could not delegate such power to the President, so the ban was void.

The scope of presidential power is a bit vague in the Constitution. The Framers assumed that the legislature would be the more influential of the two branches. Over the years, however, the authority of the executive branch has grown. In this case, the Court ruled that although the U.S. Constitution did not specifically give the President such authority, unnamed powers are inherent in the President's constitutional role as commander in chief and chief executive.

Opinion of the Court, Justice George Sutherland

. . . [T]he very delicate, plenary [full] and exclusive power of the President as the sole organ of the federal government in the field of international relations is a power which does not require as a basis for its exercise an act of Congress, but which, of course, like every other governmental power, must be exercised in subordination to the applicable provisions of the United States Constitution. If, in the maintenance of international relations, embarrassment–perhaps serious embarrassment–is to be avoided and success for national aims achieved, congressional legislation which is to be made effective through negotiation and inquiry within the international field must often accord to the President a degree of discretion and freedom from statutory [legal] restriction which would not be admissible were domestic affairs alone involved. Moreover, he, not Congress, has the better opportunity of knowing the conditions which prevail in foreign countries, and especially is this true in time of war. He has his confidential sources of information. He has his agents in the form of diplomatic, consular and other officials. Secrecy in respect of information gathered by them may be highly necessary, and the premature disclosure of it productive of harmful results.

1. According to the Court's Opinion, why doesn't the President need congressional permission to conduct foreign affairs?

2. What is the impact of this decision on the principle of separation of powers created by the Framers?

PRIMARY SOURCE

Document: *Journal of William Maclay*

The U.S. Constitution outlines the framework for a new government, but there were many other details to be hammered out before this framework was complete. Every policy decision made by Congress was unprecedented, and a whole host of governmental procedures needed to be set up, from organizing a federal judicial system to more mundane concerns, like how to address the President.

William Maclay was one of the first two senators from Pennsylvania. Sessions of the Senate were not open to the public at this time, so his diary gives a rare look at our government during the First Congress, which sat from 1789 to 1791.

30th April, Thursday
He [Vice President John Adams] rose in the most solemn manner. . . . "Gentlemen, I wish for the direction of the Senate. The President will, I suppose, address the Congress. How shall I behave? How shall we receive it? Shall it be standing or sitting?"
[May 8th]
. . . and now Mr. Elsworth moved for the report of the Joint Committee to be taken up on the subject of titles [for the President]. —It was done accordingly. Mr. Lee led the business. He took his old ground—all the world, . . . called for titles. . . . Here he began to enumerate many nations who gave titles. . . .
I collected myself for a last effort. I read the clause in the Constitution against titles of nobility. . . .
. . . "Excellency" was moved for as a title by Mr. Izard. It was withdrawn by Mr. Izard, and "highness". . . proposed by Mr. Lee. Now long harangues [ranting speeches] were made in favor of this title. . . . The debate lasted till half after three o'clock and it ended in appointing a committee to consider of a title to be given to the President. . . .
May 9th
. . . At length the committee came in and reported a title—*His Highness the President of the United States and Protector of the Rights of the Same.*

1. How efficient was Congress at resolving the issue of titles?

2. Why do you think the Vice President was so concerned with procedure and titles?

Lesson 1 An Overview of the Constitution

CLOSE READING

An Outline of the U.S. Constitution

1. **Determine Meaning of Words** Read the first paragraph under "Amendments." What does *cumbersome* mean? How would the U.S. Constitution be different if it included "cumbersome provisions," and how might this affect its longevity?

Article I

2. **Summarize** Use the graphic organizer to summarize historical, practical, and theoretical reasons why the Constitution establishes a bicameral legislature.

Reasons	Summary
Historical	
Practical	
Theoretical	

Article II

3. **Explain an Argument** The Framers debated two very different views of the presidency and how much power one person should have. Describe each argument. Which viewpoint is reflected in the Constitution?

Article III

4. **Compare and Contrast** What is the key difference between the constitutional courts and the special courts?

Basic Principles

5. **Determine Central Ideas** As you read, list each of the three basic principles included in this text, and describe the central idea of each in your own words.

6. **Draw Conclusions** In what way do citizens of today exercise popular sovereignty, and how do their actions provide an accurate reflection of the will of the citizens across the entire country?

More Basic Principles

7. **Determine Central Ideas** As you read, list each of the three basic principles included in this text, and describe each in your own words.

8. **Use Visual Information** Refer to the Checks and Balances chart. How can the U.S. President directly affect the legislative and judicial branches of government? What can the legislature do if it does not agree with the President's selection of a judge?

Lesson 2 Amending the Constitution

CLOSE READING

Formal Amendment Process

1. **Identify Key Steps** For each formal method through which the Constitution can be amended, what are the steps of the process?

2. **Identify Supporting Details** Describe the method used to adopt 26 of the 27 amendments to the Constitution. Include evidence from the text to support your answer.

Federalism and Popular Sovereignty

3. **Cite Evidence** How does the formal amendment process illustrate the goals of the Framers? What requirements of the formal amendment process support your answer?

4. **Draw Inferences** Why do you think that a State legislature might want to call for an advisory vote by the people before it ratifies an amendment proposed by Congress?

Proposing an Amendment

5. **Identify Cause and Effect** Why do you think only 27 amendments have been added to the Constitution since its ratification, even though thousands have been proposed?

The 27 Amendments

6. **Summarize** Review the 27 amendments in the reading. In your own words, write the subject of each amendment to complete the chart.

Amendments	Subject	Amendments	Subject
1–10		19	
11		20	
12		21	
13		22	
14		23	
15		24	
16		25	
17		26	
18		27	

Change by Other Means

7. **Cite Evidence** How has the interpretation of the Constitution changed through the actions of the executive and judicial branches and by party practices and customs? Use evidence from the text to support your answer.

Lesson 3 Federalism: Powers Divided

CLOSE READING

The Founders Choose Federalism

1. **Compare and Contrast** Compare the Framers' beliefs about local self-government to their attitude toward a strong central government.

What Is Federalism?

2. **Summarize** In your own words, provide a brief summary of federalism in the United States.

Three Types of Federal Powers

3. **Categorize** Complete the chart with examples of the expressed, inherent, and implied powers of the National Government.

Expressed Powers	Inherent Powers	Implied Powers

Powers Denied to the Federal Government

4. **Use Visual Information** Look at the "Examples of Powers Expressly Denied to the Federal Government" chart. Use your own words to explain why the Federal Government should be denied those powers.

Powers of the Fifty States

5. **Paraphrase** In your own words, describe the breadth of the powers reserved to the States.

The Exclusive and the Concurrent Powers

6. **Determine Meaning of Words** Explain the meaning of the phrase *concurrent powers*.

The Constitution Reigns Supreme

7. **Paraphrase** In your own words, paraphrase the Constitution's Supremacy Clause.

8. **Cite Evidence** Cite specific examples to describe the important role the Supremacy Clause has played in American history.

Lesson 4 The National Government and the States

CLOSE READING

The Nation's Obligations Under the Constitution

1. **Compare and Contrast** Before the States agreed to give up their war-making powers, each demanded that an attack on any one of the States would be met as an attack on all of them. Compare the significance of this guarantee today to its significance at the time the Constitution was written.

Admitting New States

2. **Summarize** In your own words, summarize the process used to admit new States to the United States.

States and Federal Government Sharing Resources

3. **Categorize** A State received one grant-in-aid for "health," one for "wastewater treatment," and one to conduct research on a treatment for uterine cancer. Categorize these three grants as project, categorical, or block grants in the table below. Then, write another example of each type of grant.

Project Grant	Categorical Grant	Block Grant

4. Compare and Contrast Compare the two perspectives on whether grants-in-aid support or undermine our Federal Government.

Agreements Among States

5. Determine Central Ideas Why was it necessary to establish formal procedures for making agreements among or between States?

How the Law Crosses State Lines

6. Paraphrase In your own words, explain the meaning of the phrase *Full Faith and Credit*.

Extradition

7. Determine Meaning of Words Define the word *extradition*.

Privileges and Immunities

8. Identify Supporting Details Explain the function and use of the Privileges and Immunities Clause.

PRIMARY SOURCES

Speech, Article: Two Viewpoints on the Equal Rights Amendment

Following the method used for most amendments to the U.S. Constitution, the Equal Rights Amendment (ERA) was proposed in 1972 by a two-thirds vote in each house of Congress. It then had to be approved by three-fourths of the State legislatures. It was ultimately defeated in 1982 by being a mere 3 States short of the 38 States required by the ratification deadline. The ERA, which would guarantee equal rights regardless of sex, was controversial, especially among women, largely because its goal and outcomes were interpreted differently by different groups. This discord played a role in the amendment's defeat.

Speech to the House of Representatives: "For the Equal Rights Amendment," Representative Shirley Chisholm, August 10, 1970

Mr. Speaker, House Joint Resolution 264, before us today, which provides for equality under the law for both men and women, represents one of the most clear-cut opportunities we are likely to have to declare our faith in the principles that shaped our Constitution. It provides a legal basis for attack on the most subtle, most pervasive, and most institutionalized form of prejudice that exists. Discrimination against women, solely on the basis of their sex. . . .

The amendment is necessary to clarify countless ambiguities and inconsistencies in our legal system. . . .

State labor laws applying only to women, such as those limiting hours of work and weights to be lifted, would become inoperative unless the legislature amended them to apply to men. . . .

The selective service law would have to include women, but women would not be required to serve in the Armed Forces where they are not fitted any more than men are required to serve. . . .

If any labor laws applying only to women still remained, their amendment or repeal would provide opportunity for women in better-paying jobs in manufacturing. More opportunities in public vocational and graduate schools for women would also tend to open up opportunities in better jobs for women. . . .

The focusing of public attention on the gross legal, economic, and social discrimination against women . . . would result in changes in attitude of parents, educators, and employers that would bring about substantial economic changes. . . .

This is what it comes down to: artificial distinctions between persons must be wiped out of the law. Legal discrimination between the sexes is, in almost every instance, founded on outmoded views of society and the pre-scientific beliefs about psychology and physiology. It is time to sweep away these relics of the past and set future generations free of them.

Article: "What's Wrong with 'Equal Rights' for Women?," Phyllis Schlafly, *The Report*, February 1972

In the last couple of years, a noisy movement has sprung up agitating for "women's rights." Suddenly, everywhere we are afflicted with aggressive females on television talk shows yapping about how mistreated American women are, suggesting that marriage has put us in some kind of "slavery," that housework is menial and degrading, and—perish the thought—that women are discriminated against. . . .

It's time to set the record straight. The claim that American women are downtrodden and unfairly treated is the fraud of the century. The truth is that American women never had it so good. . . .

This Amendment will absolutely and positively make women subject to the draft. Why any woman would support such a ridiculous and un-American proposal as this is beyond comprehension. . . . Fox holes are bad enough for men, but they certainly are not the place for women—and we should reject any proposal which would put them in there in the name of "equal rights." . . .

Another bad effect of the Equal Rights Amendment is that it will abolish a woman's right to child support and alimony, and substitute what the women's libbers think is a more "equal" policy, that "such decisions should be within the discretion of the Court and should be made on the economic situation and need of the parties in the case.". . .

Passage of the Equal Rights Amendment would open up a Pandora's box of trouble for women. It would deprive the American woman of many of the fundamental special privileges we now enjoy, and especially the greatest rights of all: (1) NOT to take a job, (2) to keep her baby, and (3) to be supported by her husband. . . .

Women's libbers do *not* speak for the majority of American women. American women do *not* want to be liberated from husbands and children. We do *not* want to trade our birthright of the special privileges of American women—for the mess of pottage [nonsense] called the Equal Rights Amendment.

---

1. What is the common thread among Chisholm's arguments that justify amending the U.S. Constitution?

2. How are the tones of the two sources different? Why do you think this is the case?

3. Schlafly's efforts have been credited for helping defeat the ERA. Why do you think this is the case?

PRIMARY SOURCE

Document: Letter to Congress Supporting Puerto Rico Statehood Admission Act, March 18, 2021

In 1898, Puerto Rico was acquired by the United States following the Spanish-American War. It has remained a U.S. territory ever since. Although U.S. citizenship was granted to Puerto Ricans in 1917, they are represented by only one non-voting member of the House, have no representation in the Senate, and cannot vote in presidential elections. For decades, efforts have been made for the Commonwealth to become the 51st State. In 2021, a letter was sent to Congress from the leadership of 51 organizations, including 44 that are based in Puerto Rico, urging Congress to support Puerto Rico's statehood.

For over one-hundred years, the U.S. citizens of Puerto Rico have been disenfranchised in federal elections and subjected to unequal treatment across federal programs. Last November [2020], voters stood up to change that when an absolute majority of 53% demanded statehood in a locally sponsored referendum. The Puerto Rico Statehood Admission Act, H.R. 1522 and S. 780, directly respond to that mandate, and we urge you to support it and help get it approved as soon as possible.

Puerto Rico's referendum was historic because it is the first time that statehood received unquestionable majority support on the island with a simple "YES" or "NO" vote. The 117th Congress is therefore presented with a unique opportunity to make history and put an end to America's inherently colonial rule over Puerto Rico, which runs counter to America's values of democracy, equal justice under the law, and government by the consent of the governed. . . .

Puerto Ricans stateside also favor statehood by wide margins. For example, recent polls show 81% of Puerto Rican residents in Florida and 69% of those in New York favor the admission of the island as a state. A majority of Americans have also supported the idea for decades. . . .

The only legislative option that respects the will of the people of Puerto Rico, and ensures a binding process of self-determination is . . . the Puerto Rico Statehood Admission Act. By offering statehood, stipulating the terms of admission, and requiring a ratification vote, Congress would finally open the door to full equality and democracy for the U.S. citizens of Puerto Rico while leaving the ultimate choice in their hands.

1. Which phrases were most likely included in the letter to instill a patriotic and empathetic response from Americans as well as members of Congress to the plight of Puerto Ricans?

2. How might the data quoted in the letter be used to support the opposition of Puerto Rico's statehood?

Lesson 1 National Legislature Overview

CLOSE READING

The Role of Congress in a Democracy

1. **Vocabulary: Determine Meaning** "The history of the present King of Britain," wrote Thomas Jefferson in the Declaration of Independence, "is a history of repeated injuries and usurpations, all having in direct object the establishment of an absolute tyranny over these States."

   What do you think the word *usurpations* means? What impact did this view of King George III's rule have on the form of government that emerged from the Declaration of Independence? Use evidence from the text to support your answer.

2. **Determine Author's Point of View** Use this concept web to take notes on the roles and voting options of members of Congress.

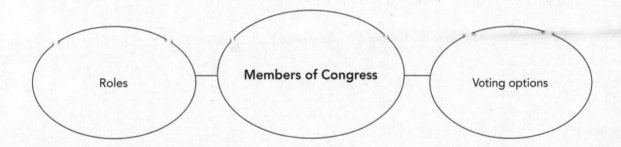

Congress: The Job

3. **Support a Point of View with Evidence** Use the text to write an opinion about the extent to which the composition of Congress *should* reflect that of the general population.

Terms and Sessions of Congress

4. Use Visual Information Refer to the text and the timeline. What is the relationship between terms and sessions of Congress? Why do you think the Framers established sessions of Congress?

5. Draw Conclusions In what ways are checks and balances applied to sessions of Congress?

Congressional Compensation

6. Paraphrase The late Senator Russell Long (D., Louisiana) characterized Congress's constitutional right to fix its own pay as "a power that no good man would want and no bad man should have." What do you think he meant?

7. Draw Conclusions How and why did the 27th Amendment modify the authority of Congress to set its own pay?

Lesson 2 The Two Houses

CLOSE READING

The House

1. **Determine Author's Point of View** Thomas Jefferson, in a conversation with George Washington, expressed his opposition to a two-chambered legislature, while pouring his coffee into a saucer to cool it. Pointing out the similarity to the purpose of the two-chambered legislature, George Washington replied, "…we pour legislation into the senatorial saucer to cool it."

   What do you think George Washington meant? Consider this quotation, and the information in the text, as you answer this question: How does the distribution of Senate seats among the States illustrate the principle of federalism?

Reapportionment of Congress

2. **Make Inferences** Study the map on reapportionment. What overall trends in population movement are seen? What is the significance of census results for each State's congressional districts?

House Elections

3. **Draw Conclusions** In the 1994 midterm election, the Democratic party lost 52 seats in the House, down to 206 seats total, and 8 seats in the Senate, down to 45 seats total. What effect do you think this had on the Democratic President's legislative agenda?

Qualifications for Office in the House

4. **Support a Point of View with Evidence** Of the different informal qualifications for membership in the House mentioned in the text, which do you think are most significant in obtaining a seat?

5. **Infer** Read the text about the events detailing the political career of Victor L. Berger of Wisconsin. What can you infer about the democratic process from this series of events?

The Senate: Size, Election, and Terms

6. **Analyze Charts** Study the chart on the growth of the membership of the House and Senate. What factors influenced the growth of the Senate and the House? What could account for the time periods when the greatest number of seats were added to the Senate and the House?

Qualifications for Office in the Senate

7. **Compare and Contrast** Compare and contrast the constitutional, as well as customary, requirements for the House and Senate using the Venn diagram below. What do you think the Framers intended in differentiating the requirements? Do you agree?

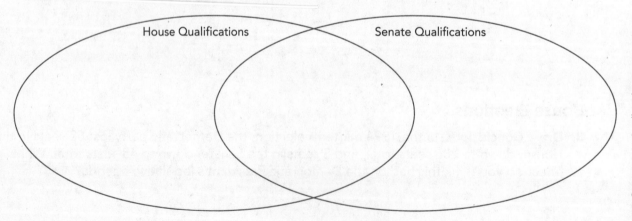

House Qualifications   Senate Qualifications

Lesson 3 The Expressed Powers

CLOSE READING

Types of Congressional Powers

1. **Identify Supporting Details** Under "Types of Congressional Powers," what details support the idea that government in the United States is a limited government and that the American system of government is federal in form?

The Commerce Power

2. **Draw Inferences** Read the section on *Gibbons* v. *Ogden,* 1824. Consider the possible effects if the Supreme Court had ruled in Ogden's favor, instead of siding with Gibbons. List examples from the text that might have resulted in different outcomes if this had been the case.

3. **Draw Inferences** Read "Limits on the Commerce Power." Why do you think the Framers placed each of the first three limits on the use of the commerce power?

The Money Powers

4. **Identify Supporting Details** As you read "The Money Powers," use this table to record information about each of the money powers that Congress is granted.

The Money Powers

Power	What May Congress Do?	What Limits are Placed on Congress?	Examples
Taxing			
Borrowing			
Bankruptcy			
Currency			

Other Domestic Powers

5. **Compare and Contrast** How are copyrights and patents similar? How are they different? Cite examples from the text to support your answer.

6. **Draw Conclusions** Some believe that the U.S. Postal Service should be abolished because its functions could be performed more efficiently by private, for-profit mail companies. Do you agree or disagree? Explain.

Congress and Foreign Policy

7. **Draw Inferences** Read the first paragraph of "Congress and Foreign Policy." How might the foreign policy of the United States be different if the Constitution had not forbidden the individual States from making treaties or alliances with foreign powers?

The War Powers

8. **Cite Evidence** The constitutionality of the War Powers Resolution remains in dispute. Explain this resolution. Do you think it is constitutional? Why or why not?

Lesson 4 The Implied and Nonlegislative Powers

CLOSE READING

The Necessary and Proper Clause

1. **Draw Conclusions** What is the Necessary and Proper Clause? Explain how this clause gives Congress flexibility in lawmaking.

2. **Assess an Argument** Congress has used the Necessary and Proper Clause to establish a minimum wage. Use evidence from the text to describe the positions a strict constructionist and a liberal constructionist would take in response to this action.

The Doctrine in Practice

3. **Draw Conclusions** Why is the Commerce Clause, written in 1787, still adequate to meet the needs of the 21st century? Cite an example from the text to support your reasoning.

The Power to Investigate

4. **Make Connections** Review the five reasons why Congress may choose to conduct investigations. Which reason(s) do you think justified the Senate investigation of intelligence agencies beginning in 1975 referenced in the text? Explain.

Executive Powers

5. **Use Visual Information** Look at the chart that summarizes congressional influence on the President's treaty-making power. Summarize the various ways Congress can influence the treaties that the President negotiates, and discuss whether or not the Framers intended Congress to wield such influence.

Impeachment

6. **Identify Supporting Details** As you read "Impeachment," use this table to record information about the four presidential impeachment cases.

The Four Presidential Impeachment Cases

President	Year	Offenses	House Actions	Senate Actions	Result

Other Powers

7. **Draw Inferences** Explain why Congress has the ultimate authority to override the President on many matters or propose amendments to the Constitution.

Lesson 5 Congress at Work—Organization and Committees

CLOSE READING

Congress Convenes

1. **Draw Inferences** During the opening day of Congress, the House of Representatives adopts the rules that will govern its proceedings through the new term. Why do you think that in 2009, the rules were amended to repeal a limit on the number of terms that any member can chair any House committee?

The Presiding Officers

2. **Draw Inferences** Why do you think that neither the Constitution nor the rules of the House require the Speaker of the House to be chosen from among the members of the House or from the majority party?

Party Officers

3. **Draw Inferences** Why do you think party officers are chosen during the party's caucus, before the Opening Day, in both the House and the Senate?

4. **Draw Conclusions** Why is it important that the party whips learn how many members will be present for a vote and how members are voting on a particular topic?

Committee Chairs

5. Assess an Argument Do you agree with the seniority rule? Why or why not?

Standing Committees

6. Draw Conclusions Why is the House Rules Committee often described as the "traffic cop" in the House of Representatives?

Select Committees

7. Explain an Argument Do you agree with the congressional power to investigate given to select committees? Why or why not?

Joint and Conference Committees

8. Summarize Briefly describe the roles of the joint and conference committees. Why is it important that these committees exist in our legislative branch?

Lesson 6 Congress at Work—Making Laws

CLOSE READING

The First Steps

1. **Check Understanding** Each session of Congress considers many different types of legislation. Choose how to classify each of the issues in the table below by using the following list: public bill, private bill, joint resolution, concurrent resolution, and simple resolution.

Description	Legislation type
An amendment to the Constitution prohibiting citizens from carrying assault weapons	
A statement of support for the government of Haiti's efforts to rebuild after the earthquake	
A proposal to require universities to pay taxes	
A requirement that a roll call be taken for all votes in the House	
A proposal for an interstate highway to take a rancher's land by eminent domain	
A declaration of war against Germany	

The Bill in Committee

2. **Apply Concepts** If you are the sponsor of a bill, what can you do to keep it from being pigeonholed?

Scheduling Floor Debate

3. **Make Decisions** You are part of a special committee to streamline procedures in the House of Representatives. Your first task is to reorganize the calendar for scheduling floor debate. Describe one major change you would make, and explain how it would streamline the legislative process.

The Bill on the House Floor

4. **Draw Conclusions** How does the Committee of the Whole help the House of Representatives manage debates?

The Bill on the Senate Floor

5. **Check Understanding** How does a filibuster protect the minority party?

House-Senate Conference Committees

6. **Explain** Why is a bill that is approved by one chamber of Congress likely to be approved by the other without change?

The President Acts on a Bill

7. **Hypothesize** If the legislature best represents the voice of the people, why does the Constitution require the President to act on bills and resolutions passed by Congress?

Unorthodox Lawmaking and Emergency Legislation

8. **Draw Inferences** In a vote on a national emergency, why are members of Congress held more accountable for an unpopular decision than the President, who is also elected by citizens?

PRIMARY SOURCE

Supreme Court Case:
Shaw v. Reno, 1993

Legal battles over voting districts became frequent after the Voting Rights Act of 1965 was enacted. By redrawing congressional districts in certain ways for partisan benefit, the political party that controlled a State legislature could ensure its political advantage. In this 1993 case, the Court held that a North Carolina redistricting plan with oddly shaped districts indicated possible racial gerrymandering and accordingly deserved strict scrutiny by the courts.

Majority Opinion, Justice Sandra Day O'Connor

. . . This case involves two of the most complex and sensitive issues this Court has faced in recent years: the meaning of the constitutional "right" to vote, and the propriety of race-based state legislation designed to benefit members of historically disadvantaged racial minority groups. . . . Appellants allege that the revised plan, . . . constitutes an unconstitutional racial gerrymander.

. . . When a district obviously is created solely to effectuate the perceived common interests of one racial group, elected officials are more likely to believe that their primary obligation is to represent only the members of that group, rather than their constituency as a whole. This is altogether antithetical to our system of representative democracy.

. . . racial classifications receive close scrutiny even when they may be said to burden or benefit the races equally.

. . . the very reason that the Equal Protection Clause demands strict scrutiny of all racial classifications is because without it, a court cannot determine whether or not the discrimination truly is "benign."

Racial classifications of any sort pose the risk of lasting harm to our society. They reinforce the belief, held by too many for too much of our history, that individuals should be judged by the color of their skin. Racial classifications with respect to voting carry particular dangers. Racial gerrymandering, even for remedial purposes, may balkanize [divide into small quarrelsome blocs] us into competing racial factions; it threatens to carry us further from the goal of a political system in which race no longer matters—a goal that the Fourteenth and Fifteenth Amendments embody, and to which the Nation continues to aspire. It is for these reasons that race-based districting by our state legislatures demands close judicial scrutiny.

1. Why did the Court rule that racial classifications could not be used to determine voting districts, even if they benefit the races equally?

2. How does the Equal Protection Clause apply to this case?

Speech: "Communists in Our Government," Joseph McCarthy, Wheeling, West Virginia, February 9, 1950

In the early 1950s, Wisconsin Senator Joseph McCarthy gained widespread support by capitalizing on the fears of Americans over the spread of communism in eastern Europe, Korea, and China. He presided over investigations of various government departments, accusing so-called traitors within the State Department of allowing communism to spread. His unfounded accusations caused his targets to be blacklisted. A blacklist is a list privately exchanged among employers, containing the names of persons to be barred from employment because of untrustworthiness or for holding opinions considered undesirable. Hundreds of people's careers and reputations were destroyed as a result. This intimidation of people to conform and/or denounce others became known as *McCarthyism*.

In this speech, McCarthy accused the State Department of harboring collaborators.

. . . [T]his is not a period of peace. This is a time of "the cold war." This is a time when all the world is split into two vast, increasingly hostile armed camps. . .

. . . [W]e are now engaged in a show-down fight . . . not the usual war between nations for land areas or other material gains, but a war between two diametrically opposed ideologies [belief system that guides actions].

The great difference between our western Christian world and the atheistic [deny existence of supreme being] Communist world is not political, gentlemen, it is moral.

The reason why we find ourselves in a position of impotency [weakness] is not because our only powerful potential enemy has sent men to invade our shores . . . but rather because of the traitorous actions of those who have been treated so well by this Nation. . . .

In my opinion the State Department, which is one of the most important government departments, is thoroughly infested with communists.

I have in my hand 205 cases of individuals who would appear to be either card-carrying members or certainly loyal to the Communist Party, but who nevertheless are still helping to shape our foreign policy.

[The moral uprising of the American people]. . . will end only when the whole sorry mess of twisted warped thinkers are swept from the national scene so that we may have a new birth of national honesty and decency in government.

1. Whom does Senator McCarthy blame for the spread of communism?

2. How and why does McCarthy portray the Cold War as different from usual wars?

PRIMARY SOURCE

Speech: "Declaration of Conscience," Margaret Chase Smith, June 1, 1950

Senator Margaret Chase Smith of Maine was one of the first Senators to take a public stand against Senator McCarthy's tactics, at great personal risk. In this speech to the Senate, she condemned his anticommunist witch hunts, attacking him without ever mentioning his name. She criticized both parties for not taking a stand against his baseless attacks and fear-mongering.

Mr. President, I would like to speak briefly and simply about a serious national condition. It is a national feeling of fear and frustration . . . It is a condition that comes from the lack of effective leadership either in the legislative branch or the executive branch of our government. . . .

Mr. President, I speak as a Republican. I speak as a woman. I speak as a United States senator. I speak as an American. . . .

The United States Senate has long enjoyed worldwide respect as the greatest deliberative body in the world. But recently that deliberative character has too often been debased to the level of a forum of hate and character assassination sheltered by the shield of congressional immunity. . . .

Those of us who shout the loudest about Americanism in making character assassinations are all too frequently those who, by our own words and acts, ignore some of the basic principles of Americanism—

The right to criticize.

The right to hold unpopular beliefs.

The right to protest.

The right of independent thought.

. . . Freedom of speech is not what it used to be in America. It has been so abused by some that it is not exercised by others. . . .

As a United States senator, I am not proud of the way in which the Senate has been made a publicity platform for irresponsible sensationalism. . . .

As an American, I want to see our nation recapture the strength and unity it once had when we fought the enemy instead of ourselves.

It is with these thoughts that I have drafted what I call a Declaration of Conscience.

1. We are Republicans. But we are Americans first. It is as Americans that we express our concern with the growing confusion that threatens the security and stability of our country. Democrats and Republicans alike have contributed to that confusion. . . .

5. It is high time that we stopped thinking politically as Republicans and Democrats about elections and started thinking patriotically as Americans about national security based on individual freedom. It is high time that we all stopped being tools and victims of totalitarian techniques—techniques that, if continued here unchecked, will surely end what we have come to cherish as the American way of life.

---

1. Cite passages in Senator Chase's speech in which she criticizes the Senate.

2. How does Senator Chase personalize her views and try to get the support of other senators?

Lesson 1 The Presidency—An Overview

CLOSE READING

The President's Many Roles

1. **Summarize** As you read "The President's Many Roles," use this graphic organizer to keep track of the presidential roles and the responsibilities each entails. Use your completed outline to analyze the ways in which the expectations for the additional presidential roles differ from those that are specified by the Constitution.

I. The President's Roles—Constitutional
    A. Chief of state
        1. _____
        2. _____
    B. _____
        1. _____
        2. _____
    C. _____
        1. _____
        2. _____
    D. _____
        1. _____
        2. _____
    E. _____
        1. _____
        2. _____
    F. _____
        1. _____
        2. _____
    G. _____
        1. _____
        2. _____
    H. _____
        1. _____
        2. _____
    I. _____
        1. _____
        2. _____

2. **Cite Evidence** As you've read, in many countries, the chief of state reigns but does not rule. Cite evidence from your reading on the President's many roles to support the statement that the President of the United States both reigns and rules.

Qualifications for the Presidency

3. **Draw Conclusions** What are the formal qualifications for the office of the President, and why do you think the Framers specified these requirements?

4. **Draw Inferences** In an upcoming campaign, two candidates want to run for President. Their qualifications are as follows:

Candidate A
- 47 years old
- college graduate
- lived in the United States through college; currently living and working in Italy
- born in the United States

Candidate B
- 54 years old
- attended college, but didn't graduate
- born in France to American citizens
- moved to United States at age 20; has lived here since that time

Which candidate might have his or her candidacy questioned based on which constitutional provision?

The Presidential Term of Office

5. **Compare and Contrast** In what way did George Washington and Franklin D. Roosevelt differ in their approaches to presidential term limits? How were those beliefs reflected in their presidencies? With which of these two men would President Reagan have agreed?

Presidential Succession and Disability

6. **Summarize** In what way did the Presidential Succession Act of 1947 and the 25th Amendment clarify the Constitution's handling of presidential vacancies?

7. **Cite Evidence** What is the "disability gap," and why was it important that it be filled? Include at least one example from the reading to support your answer.

Lesson 2 The Vice President and the First Lady

CLOSE READING

The Structure and Function of the Vice Presidency

1. Summarize Use this chart to organize information from this text.

	Vice President
How does this person come into office?	
Where is this person in the line of presidential succession?	
What are some responsibilities of this office?	

2. Vocabulary: Use Context Clues Read the second paragraph of "Early Vice Presidents." What do you think the word *superfluous* means? Why do you think Benjamin Franklin thought the Vice President was *superfluous*? Use evidence from the text to support your answer.

3. Draw Inferences Read the quotation from Thomas Marshall in the section "Early Vice Presidents." How might a recent Vice President, such as Dick Cheney or Joe Biden, respond to this quotation?

4. **Identify Cause and Effect** Look at the image in the text that shows the testing of an atomic bomb in 1945. In what way did this event affect the role of the Vice President?

The First Lady

5. **Summarize** Select two First Ladies who were discussed in the text, and explain how each approached her role as First Lady. Discuss the impact each made on the role. Use evidence from the text to support your answer.

6. **Determine Author's Point of View**

   "This was I and yet not I, this was the wife of the President of the United States and she took precedence over me; my personal likes and dislikes must be subordinated to the consideration of those things which were required of her."

   —*First Lady Grace Coolidge, wife of President Calvin Coolidge*

   Reflect on these words from First Lady Grace Coolidge. What do they say about the role of the First Lady?

Lesson 3 The President's Domestic Powers

CLOSE READING

The Growth of Presidential Power

1. **Identify Supporting Details** Use the graphic organizer to identify the reasons for the growth of presidential power.

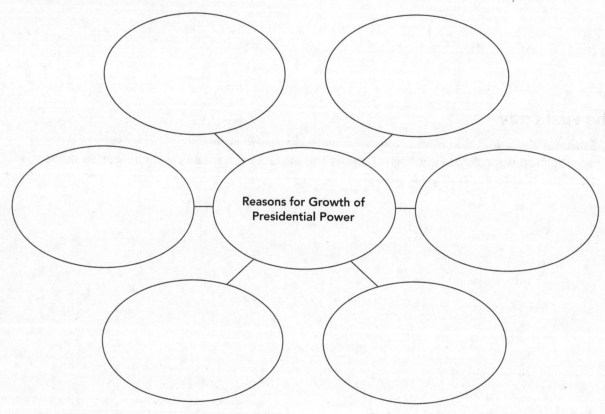

Reasons for Growth of Presidential Power

The Power to Execute the Law

2. **Draw Inferences** Immigration laws require that all immigrants seeking permanent admission to the United States must be able to "read and understand some dialect or language." The U.S. Citizenship and Immigration Services decides how well immigrants must be able to "read and understand." How is this situation an example of the separation of powers between the legislative and executive branches?

Executive Orders and Executive Privilege

3. **Determine Central Ideas** Does the idea of executive privilege safeguard or disrupt the separation of powers between the executive and the legislative branches?

The Powers of Appointment and Removal

4. Draw Inferences Consider this statement: The unwritten rule of senatorial courtesy contradicts the principle of separation of powers. Do you agree or disagree? Explain why.

The Powers of Clemency

5. Assess an Argument The judicial powers of the President help maintain the system of checks and balances in the government. Do you agree with this statement? Why or why not?

The Power to Recommend Legislation

6. Identify Cause and Effect How does the role of chief legislator help the President contribute to the creation of new federal laws?

The Power of the Veto

7. Determine Central Ideas How might the line-item veto increase the legislative powers of the President?

Lesson 4 The President's Foreign Affairs Powers

CLOSE READING

The President's Diplomatic Powers

1. **Summarize** In negotiations with another sovereign state, the President sometimes makes a treaty but other times signs an executive agreement. Use the graphic organizer to list the major features of each.

Treaty	Executive Agreement

2. **Identify Key Steps** When the Senate does not approve a treaty, what measures can the President take to maneuver around this type of check and balance of power? Use an example from the reading in your answer.

3. **Infer** In 1933, President Franklin D. Roosevelt formally recognized the Soviet Union. During the Cold War of the 1950s and 1960s, military threats between the United States and the Soviet Union escalated, but the United States did not withdraw its recognition of that country. Why would a President want to continue recognizing a country when it has expressed hostility towards the United States?

4. **Determine Central Ideas** In the treaty-making process, how do the President and Congress act as checks and balances on each other? Can Congress ever repeal a treaty? Can the President use a treaty to repeal a law? When do the courts get involved in treaties?

Commander in Chief

5. **Use Visual Information** Look at the photograph of President Abraham Lincoln visiting United States troops during the Civil War. What authority did President Lincoln have to talk to soldiers in the field? How might these visits have helped the war effort?

6. **Analyze Interactions** The United States has not declared war against another country since 1942, yet it has been involved in several military actions since then. Name one of these actions. Did Congress and the President work together to support this undeclared war? Explain.

7. **Analyze Interactions** The War Powers Resolution of 1973 gives the President the power to order troops into combat when the United States is directly attacked. Why, then, did Congress need to pass a special resolution allowing the President to use force against the nations involved in the terror attacks of September 11, 2001?

PRIMARY SOURCE

Narrative: *The Land of Hope: An Invitation to the Great American Story* by Wilfred M. McClay

The President largely decides what is in the best interest of the United States in foreign affairs. The President can use negotiations, and, at times, military force, to carry out goals. However, the checks and balances system ensures oversight on policies related to both domestic and foreign affairs.

The *Lusitania* affair had contributed to a growing consensus among a wide range of Americans that a heightened and improved level of military preparedness was now an imperative task for the nation. After some resistance, Wilson himself was won over to this point of view and persuaded Congress to pass legislation to increase the size of the army to a (still very small) 175,000 and authorize the construction of some fifty new warships in the coming year.

But the sinking of five unarmed U.S. merchant vessels in the first weeks of March was enough. Wilson was now ready to ask for a declaration of war, and did so on April 2, in a speech that decried Germany's submarine policy as "warfare against mankind" and declared that "the world must be made safe for democracy."

On April 6, an overwhelming majority of Congress agreed and voted yes.

In successive engagements, the Americans became more and more deeply involved, in greater and greater numbers. Finally, in late September, more than a million American troops drove west from blood-soaked Verdun along the Meuse River and then through the Argonne Forest. For a month of grisly, terrifying battle, the Americans crawled and slashed through the Argonne – rough, hilly terrain that the Germans had spent the past four years fortifying – while the French and British armies pushed against the Germans to the west, driving them back toward the German border. Finally, the Americans broke through on November 1, and the French Fourth Army was allowed the honor of recapturing Sedan (the site of a humiliating French defeat in the Franco-Prussian War). The Germans were forced to surrender and sign an armistice on November 11 – the day Americans now celebrate as Veterans Day.

Woodrow Wilson grasped all of this. He understood the gravity of the historical moment and brought to it an alternative vision to the task of postwar settlement – a vision that he believed could ensure that the Allied powers' costly victory would not turn out to have been in vain. And he was willing and eager to be the instrument by which that vision came to be reality. He had been busily consulting with experts in various fields about the optimal course of action to take when the time came to negotiate the peace treaty. He hoped that the resulting plan, his Fourteen Points, would be his most important achievement.

Wilson concluded that only the force of his personality could prevail over the entrenched forces of inertia and cynicism, and he decided that he would go in person to Paris to lead the American peace delegation.

Wilson was in the end willing to sacrifice all else to gain the final of his Fourteen Points, the "association of nations," what became the League of Nations. All else, he believed, would be possible in due course if such an organization, committed to collective security and mutual accountability, could be established.

When he rolled out a draft of his plan for the League's structure on Valentine's Day 1919, it immediately encountered stiff resistance from Republicans. Senator Henry Cabot Lodge, an inveterate foe of Wilson's who was newly elected as chairman of the powerful Senate Foreign Relations Committee – and thus would be essential to the ratification of the treaty coming out of the Paris talks – not only opposed the League but got thirty-nine Republican senators or senators-elect to sign a "round robin" opposing it and demanding that the League issue be delinked from the treaty itself, to be decided separately. It was not an unreasonable position; and even if it had been, a prudent leader would have taken account of the fact that thirty-nine senators was more than enough to block the treaty from receiving the two-thirds vote needed for ratification. Nevertheless, Wilson brushed their demands aside

Several months of political wrangling followed, in which various groups arose, with various degrees of aversion to the League.

But Wilson would not negotiate with any of them; he simply refused to consider any substantive changes

Wilson, sensing at last that the tide was not going his way, chose to fight in a place where he believed he could win: the court of public opinion. He launched into a nationwide speaking tour that would rally support for his League and put pressure on the Senate to follow suit. But it was an exercise in futility. The barnstorming tour did nothing to affect the disposition of the Senate, and finally, after delivering a powerful address at Pueblo, Colorado, Wilson collapsed, having had a massive stroke that left him partly paralyzed. He was out of the public eye for two months as he recovered, and during that time, public opinion turned decisively against the League and the treaty, which were voted down.

---

1. How involved was President Wilson in directing foreign affairs?

2. How do these passages show the limits of presidential power?

Supreme Court Case:
Clinton, President of the United States v. *City of New York*, 1998

The Line Item Veto Act of 1996 gave the President the power to amend or repeal parts of budget bills that had been passed by Congress. The law was intended to limit government spending by giving the President the right to cancel a single appropriation or tax benefit within a large appropriations or tax bill without having to veto the entire bill. President Clinton exercised this power by cancelling two provisions of the Balanced Budget Act of 1997. The law was quickly challenged. The Supreme Court ruled that the law allowed the President unilateral authority to change enacted laws and was therefore unconstitutional.

Majority Opinion, Justice John Paul Stevens

. . . There is no provision in the Constitution that authorizes the President to enact, to amend, or to repeal statutes. Both Article I and Article II assign responsibilities to the President that directly relate to the lawmaking process, but neither addresses the issue presented by these cases. . . . [The President] may initiate and influence legislative proposals. Moreover, after a bill has passed both Houses of Congress, but "before it become[s] a Law," it must be presented to the President. If he approves it, "he shall sign it, but if not he shall return it, . . . His "return" of a bill, which is usually described as a "veto," is subject to being overridden by a two-thirds vote in each House.

. . . whenever the President cancels an item of new direct spending or a limited tax benefit he is rejecting the policy judgment made by Congress and relying on his own policy judgment. . . . this Act gives the President the unilateral power to change the text of duly enacted statues.

. . . Our decision rests on the narrow ground that the procedures authorized by the Line Item Veto Act are not authorized by the Constitution. . . . If the Line Item Veto Act were valid, it would authorize the President to create a different law—one whose text was not voted on by either House of Congress or presented to the President for signature. Something that might be known as "Public Law 105-33 as modified by the President" may or may not be desirable, but it is surely not a document that may "become a law" pursuant to Article I, [Sec.] 7. If there is to be a new procedure in which the President will play a different role, such change must come through the Article V amendment procedures.

1. Why would allowing the Line Item Veto Law to be enforced upset the system of checks and balances?

2. Identify the passages in the Majority Opinion that give the basis for the Supreme Court decision.

Lesson 1 The Federal Bureaucracy

CLOSE READING

What Is a Bureaucracy?

1. **Determine Author's Point of View** Read the following quotation from Walter Bagehot from 1867:

   "A bureaucracy is sure to think that its duty is to augment [increase] official power, official business, or official members, rather than to leave free the energies of mankind; it overdoes the quantity of government, as well as impairs its quality."

   What is Bagehot's opinion of bureaucracy? How does it compare with the opinion expressed by James Madison (quoted in this lesson)?

2. **Draw Conclusions** How does bureaucracy increase the effectiveness of the Federal Government? At the same time, how does bureaucracy limit the Federal Government's effectiveness?

Executive Branch Bureaucracy

3. **Categorize** Refer to the "Executive Branch Bureaucracy" text. Show the hierarchy of organization in the executive branch of the Federal Government by completing the graphic organizer.

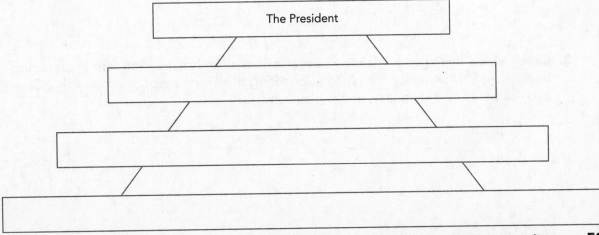

The President

4. **Identify Supporting Details** What does the Constitution say about the administration of the executive branch?

How Units Are Named

5. **Identify Supporting Details** In what way are names for government agencies common but not standardized?

6. **Draw Conclusions** Why do you think so much inconsistency exists in the names of the various government agencies?

Staff and Line Agencies

7. **Analyze Interactions** As you read "Staff and Line Agencies," make notes on how staff agencies and line agencies are different entities that work together.

8. **Categorize** The Office of Management and Budget assists the President in preparing the budget, and NASA is responsible for pioneering the future in space exploration. Categorize each as a staff or line agency, and explain why.

Lesson 2 The EOP and the Executive Departments

CLOSE READING

Structure of the Executive Office of the President

1. **Summarize** Complete the chart to show the functions of some of the agencies and advisors that are part of the Executive Office of the President.

Advisor or Agency	Function
White House Chief of Staff	
National Security Council	
Office of Management and Budget	
Office of National Drug Control Policy	
Council of Economic Advisers	
Domestic Policy Council	
Council on Environmental Quality	

The Executive Departments

2. **Draw Inferences** Why do you think it is important that the President select executive department heads?

3. **Analyze Interactions** In what ways can the chief officers and staff of the executive departments support the President's policy agenda?

4. **Cite Evidence** Each department is made up of subunits, and those subunits are composed of sections. What aspect of this structure do you think allows these departments to direct the work of staff who are located in many places across the nation? Cite evidence in the text to support your answer.

The Cabinet and Its Functions

5. **Identify Cause and Effect** The role and importance of the Cabinet has changed over time. How has it changed, and how have various Presidents contributed to those changes? Use evidence from the text to support your answer.

6. **Use Visual Information** Look at the images of Presidents Washington and Kennedy and their Cabinets. Notice their differences. How do you think the factors that Presidents consider when selecting executive department heads have changed over time?

7. **Draw Inferences** Read the quotation by William Howard Taft. What do you think the author means by the statement that "William Howard Taft put the Cabinet in its proper light"? Use evidence from the text to support your answer.

Lesson 3 The Independent Agencies

CLOSE READING

The Purpose of Independent Agencies

1. **Summarize** As you read "The Purpose of Independent Agencies," provide four reasons why Congress located the independent agencies outside of Cabinet departments. What do you think would happen if the independent agencies were located within Cabinet departments?

Independent Executive Agencies

2. **Compare and Contrast** Use the Venn diagram to compare and contrast the three types of independent agencies as you read the remainder of the texts: "Independent Executive Agencies," "Independent Regulatory Commissions," and "Government Corporations."

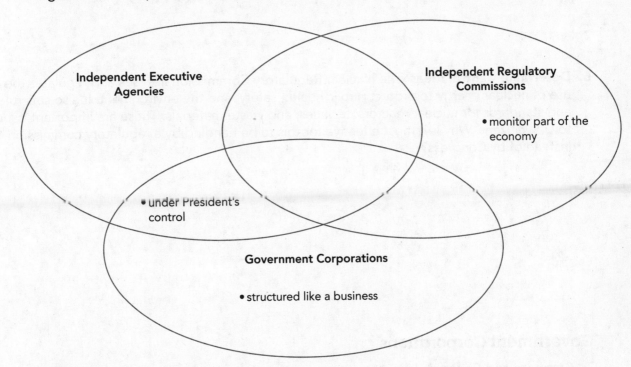

3. **Identify Cause and Effect** How has the process of selecting federal workers changed throughout our history, and what caused this change?

4. **Use Visual Information** Look at the icons in the infographic on NASA technologies. Describe these and other civilian advancements made possible by NASA's military work.

Independent Regulatory Commissions

5. **Explain an Argument** Many argue that regulatory commissions have been influenced by the special interests they are expected to regulate. Do you agree? Give an example to support your thinking.

6. **Determine Central Ideas** The Nuclear Regulatory Commission licenses and regulates the use of nuclear energy to protect public health, safety, and the environment. It also sets rules and standards for nuclear reactors, facilities, and waste materials. These are important issues to U.S. citizens. Why is it most effective for this to be handled by a regulatory commission instead of by Congress?

Government Corporations

7. **Compare and Contrast** How are government corporations similar to private corporations? How are they different?

Lesson 4 Foreign Policy Overview

CLOSE READING

What Is Foreign Policy?

1. **Use Visual Information** Read the text, and look at the images. In what ways can foreign policy influence domestic policy in the United States?

Beginnings Through World War I

2. **Draw Conclusions** In what ways did the policy of isolationism and the creation of the Monroe Doctrine shape American foreign policy in the late 1700s and early 1800s?

3. **Compare and Contrast** Why might the Roosevelt Corollary be seen as a natural extension of the Monroe Doctrine? In what way was it different from that policy?

4. **Summarize** Use information from throughout this lesson to complete the timeline and show how our relations with China have changed over time.

U.S.–China Relations

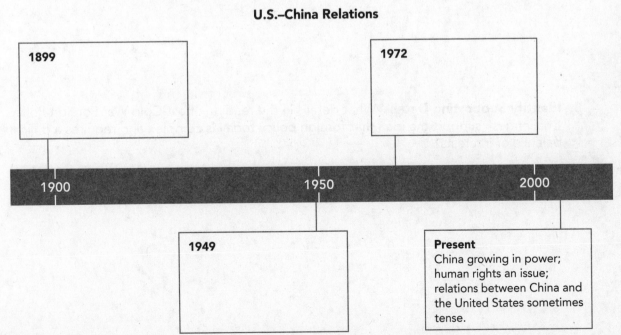

1899

1972

1900   1950   2000

1949

Present
China growing in power;
human rights an issue;
relations between China and
the United States sometimes
tense.

World War II to the End of the Cold War

5. **Identify Cause and Effect** What long-term effect did the overall shift in foreign policy away from isolationism during World War II have on America's position in the world?

6. **Summarize** Describe the different foreign policies that the United States has practiced over time with regard to the Soviet Union.

Post-Cold War Foreign Policy Challenges

7. **Distinguish Among Fact, Opinion, and Reasoned Judgment** Is it critical for the United States to continue its heavy involvement in world affairs? Write your opinion about this question. Then write one fact to support it. Finally, change your statement of opinion to one of reasoned judgment.

8. **Identify Supporting Details** What details in the reading "Post-Cold War Foreign Policy Challenges" support the idea that foreign policy today is complex and requires a delicate balance of interests?

Lesson 5 Diplomacy

CLOSE READING

America's Representatives to the World

1. **Draw Inferences** Why do you think the author describes the State Department as "the President's right arm in foreign affairs"?

American Foreign Aid

2. **Determine Central Ideas** How did America's first foreign aid programs impact the balance of world power? Cite evidence from the text to support your answer.

3. **Assess an Argument** Consider the following argument in favor of continued economic aid to other nations, and then assess its validity: Foreign economic aid to other countries is a good investment for the United States. It comprises only 1 percent of the entire federal budget, some $20 billion dollars, and yet returns untold amounts in increased sales of American goods and services.

NATO

4. **Analyze Sequence** How has NATO's composition and mission evolved over time?

The United Nations

5. **Summarize** Use the chart below to summarize the purpose and work of the UN General Assembly and Security Council. If you find any other information about these governing bodies as you read the text, add it to the row labeled "Other."

	UN General Assembly	UN Security Council
Membership		
Purpose		
Meetings		
Other		

The UN's Work

6. **Paraphrase** Use your own words to describe the overall mission of the UN.

7. **Determine Author's Point of View** What details help to explain why the author describes America's relationship with the UN as "complex"?

The Organization of American States

8. **Categorize** List the four issues that the author uses as examples of concerns of the Organization of American States. Categorize each according to whether it reflects the OAS effort to promote stability or its effort to promote cooperation among its member states.

Lesson 6 National Security

CLOSE READING

The Department of Defense

1. **Draw Inferences** How might have World War II contributed to the decision to create a single Department of Defense in 1947?

2. **Cite Evidence** Cite evidence supporting the statement that "The Framers . . . recognized the dangers inherent in military power and its abuse."

Branches of the Military

3. **Identify Cause and Effect** Why has the number of active duty soldiers in the army declined?

4. **Compare and Contrast** Complete the chart to show how the three branches of the military differ. Include information related to the age, area of operations, and mission of each branch.

Three Branches of the Military		
Army	Navy	Air Force

The Director of National Intelligence

5. **Summarize** Describe the work conducted by the Office of the Director of National Intelligence (DNI).

6. **Draw Inferences** Why do you think the budget of the DNI is disguised within the federal budget?

The Department of Homeland Security

7. **Determine Meaning of Words** Define and provide examples of terrorism.

8. **Analyze Interactions** Explain how the Department of Homeland Security operates at all levels of government, including federal, State, and local.

PRIMARY SOURCE

Document: Press Briefing by Ari Fleischer, September 12, 2001

A key position in the White House Office is that of the press secretary. He or she is the voice of the President during the press briefings conducted before the White House press corps. The press secretary provides the administration's "official comment" on recent events. The position can be extremely difficult in times of tragedy, such as the September 11, 2001 attacks against the United States. In those instances, the skill of the press secretary is greatly tested, as illustrated below by the exchange between the press corps and Ari Fleischer, who held the position during that tragic event.

Question: Ari, in terms of the President's statement this morning that this was an act of war, was it the realization that both the White House and Air Force One were targeted that elevated his language to talk about an act of war? . . .

MR. FLEISCHER: John, I think that the actions against the soil of the United States are what led the President to say that this was an act of war against the United States.

Question: But why not use the word "war" last night in his televised address to the nation? What changed overnight to ratchet up [heighten] that rhetoric?

MR. FLEISCHER: I think that you are just going to continue to hear the President speak out on a regular basis, and the President will share his thoughts with you as his thoughts develop. . . .

Question: Ari, given the President's language today, is there any discussion here of asking Congress for a declaration of war?

MR. FLEISCHER: You know, again, as the President said, there were acts of war that were carried out against our country. And the President will continue to work with Congress on any appropriate measures at the appropriate time. But, you know, this is also a different situation from situations our nation has faced in the past. . . . we are dealing, at least at this point, with nameless, faceless people. . . . So we will continue to work with the Congress on appropriate language at the appropriate time.

Question: So, just to try to understand your answer, given what you said, since it is unclear who has done this, or officially unclear who has done this at this point, is it less likely that there will be a request for a declaration of war?

MR. FLEISCHER: No, I didn't indicate one way or another. I said that the President will continue to work with Congress on appropriate language at the appropriate time.

Question: So you're not ruling it out, then?

MR. FLEISCHER: I've answered the question

1. How does this exchange illustrate the state of the nation at the time?

2. Using this excerpt, how challenging do you think it is for a press secretary to be the "voice of the President"?

PRIMARY SOURCE

Political Cartoon: Regulations by Sidney Harris

Among the aims of the independent regulatory agencies is to protect the health and well-being of consumers as well as ensure fairness and competition in the marketplace. However, the regulations these agencies establish are often criticized for being complex, confusing, and so restrictive that they inhibit economic growth.

"THE DEPT. OF AGRICULTURE SAYS YES, THE ENVIRONMENTAL PROTECTION AGENCY SAYS MAYBE, AND THE FOOD AND DRUG ADMINISTRATION SAYS NO."

1. What is the main criticism about government regulations that the cartoonist is trying to communicate?

2. Do you think it is possible that a situation similar to the one described in the cartoon might actually be beneficial to the business and the consumer?

Speech: Report on United Nations Charter, Senator Tom Connally (D., Texas), *Congressional Record*, June 28, 1945

In June 1945, Senator Thomas Connally gave a report to his colleagues in the U.S. Senate about the charter of an organization that he firmly believed would put an end to war. As the vice chairman of the United Nations Conference on International Organization, he was well acquainted with the charter and the aims of the new organization it would establish—the United Nations. Although the UN was an unknown entity at the time, Connally recognized that the organization that the charter created had the potential to change the world.

The scope of agreement reached at San Francisco has been remarkable, and notwithstanding divergent [differing] views and earnest [sincere] attachment to differing concepts, final and complete agreement was reached on the entire charter [a document creating an organization]. This was true because all the 50 nations at San Francisco aspired to [aimed for] the same sublime [outstanding] goal which called the Conference into being.

Its adoption marks an epochal [extremely significant] period in international affairs. It creates an agency of tremendous influence and power. The future course of history may be affected by its conduct and by its heroic efforts in behalf of peace. However, it creates no superstate. The rights and powers of individual states are not impaired, except to the extent of the obligations and duties which they voluntarily assume when they sign the charter. . . .

Mere documents, language, and phrases cannot themselves prevent war and preserve peace. They must rest upon the will and the purpose and the desires of the peoples and nations of the world. Organization, however, promotes these objectives. It stimulates and quickens high purposes by the knowledge that others share those ends. Enlightened and compelling world opinion in behalf of law and justice and freedom and peace will give life and vigor to documents and charters. . . .

The central idea of the charter is that the comradeship of war must be carried forward in a comradeship of peace. If we have been able to fight side by side in killing and destroying, why shall we not league [group] together to save millions of human lives and permit the people of the earth to rebuild their tortured lands and to recreate wasted wealth and shattered homes.

We leagued our armed might for war. Now let us league our moral and material might for peace.

1. What reasons does Connally give that support his argument that the UN will succeed in preventing war?

2. From a modern standpoint, would you agree with Connally's prediction that the agency the charter created has tremendous influence and power? Why or why not?

Lesson 1 The National Judiciary

CLOSE READING

The Courts and Democracy

1. **Analyze Interactions** During the years 1781–1789, when the Articles of Confederation were in still force, there was no federal court system. How were the laws of the United States interpreted and applied at that time?

Creation of a National Judiciary

2. **Cite Evidence** In *The Federalist* No. 22, Alexander Hamilton refers to a "circumstance which crowns the defects of the Confederation." What circumstance is he referring to? How can you tell that he feels strongly about this matter?

Jurisdiction in the Federal Court System

3. **Summarize** Under what circumstances do federal courts have jurisdiction in a case?

4. **Integrate Information from Diverse Sources** Read the second paragraph of "Jurisdiction in the Federal Court System." Then look at the infographic. What do the text and the infographic each tell you concerning federal court jurisdiction?

Types of Jurisdiction

5. **Analyze Interactions** What does it mean when it is said that the federal courts exercise both exclusive and concurrent jurisdiction?

6. **Identify Cause and Effect** As you read "Original and Appellate Jurisdiction," use this graphic organizer to record the three possible effects of a court with original jurisdiction sending a decision on to an appellate court.

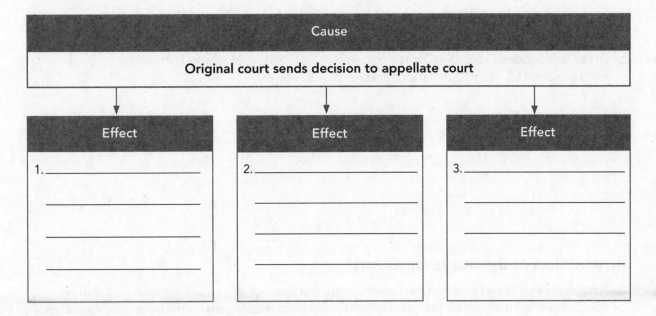

Cause
Original court sends decision to appellate court

Effect	Effect	Effect
1. _____	2. _____	3. _____
_____	_____	_____
_____	_____	_____
_____	_____	_____

Federal Judges and Court Officers

7. **Draw Inferences** What role does judicial philosophy play in the selection of judges?

8. **Identify Supporting Details** What requirements for federal judges are detailed in the Constitution?

Lesson 2 The Supreme Court

CLOSE READING

What Is Judicial Review?

1. **Analyze** Consider the interactions between the Supreme Court, William Marbury, Thomas Jefferson, and James Madison in *Marbury* v. *Madison*. How did the Court give itself more power by denying that it had the jurisdiction to hear the case?

2. **Draw Inferences** Does the Court's decision in *Marbury* v. *Madison* to exercise judicial review make U.S. democracy more stable, or less so?

Jurisdiction of the Supreme Court

3. **Paraphrase** Notice the word *exclusive* in the third paragraph of this section. Explain what it means for the Supreme Court to have original and *exclusive* jurisdiction over certain cases.

4. **Categorize** Give an example of each of the Court's two types of jurisdiction.

Appealing to the Supreme Court

5. Draw Conclusions How do justices decide whether or not to accept a case on appeal?

Hearing a Supreme Court Case

6. Draw Inferences What groups of people do you think read and follow Supreme Court decisions most closely? Why?

7. Identify Cause and Effect Why do justices write concurring and dissenting opinions? What effect do concurring and dissenting opinions have on future cases?

Lesson 3 The Inferior Courts and the Special Courts

CLOSE READING

The Structure and Role of the Federal District Courts

1. **Draw Conclusions** The daily routines of one federal district court judge might vary greatly from the routines of another. Explain why these court officials can have a common job title but very different experiences on the job.

The Structure and Role of the Federal Courts of Appeals

2. **Analyze Sequence** Read the information about a case that is given in the flowchart below. Then explain the next step in the case.

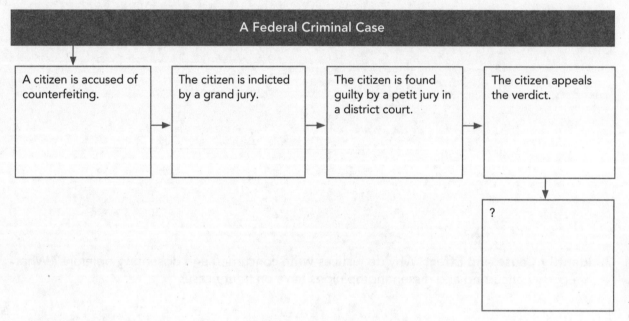

A Federal Criminal Case

A citizen is accused of counterfeiting.

The citizen is indicted by a grand jury.

The citizen is found guilty by a petit jury in a district court.

The citizen appeals the verdict.

?

3. **Compare and Contrast** Think about how cases are heard in the federal district courts vs. the federal appeals courts. If a judge describes herself as "an outgoing person who enjoys witnessing human interaction," in which of the two types of courts would she be more comfortable, and why?

The Court of International Trade

4. **Draw Inferences** Why are jury trials in the Court of International Trade often held in port cities?

Military Justice—Special Courts and Commissions

5. **Analyze Interactions** Explain how the three branches of government are or are not involved in the formation of a legitimate military commission.

6. **Categorize** Why is the Court of Appeals for Veterans Claims neither a court of first instance nor a court of final instance?

Other Special Courts

7. **Identify Cause and Effect** Describe a circumstance in which the findings of the Court of Federal Claims would be meaningless.

8. **Compare and Contrast** What does the United States Tax Court have in common with courts-martial? With the Court of International Trade?

PRIMARY SOURCE

Interview: "In Conversation with U.S. Supreme Court Justice Sonya Sotomayor," February 14, 2019

Sonia Sotomayor has had a varied legal career. She worked in New York City as an assistant to the district attorney before joining a private practice that focused on business and corporate law. She later served on the U.S. District Court and in 1997 was nominated to the United States Court of Appeals for the Second Circuit. She became an Associate on the Supreme Court in August 2009, the first Hispanic American and the third woman to serve on the High Court.

In this interview, she describes the different court levels on which she served.

SPEAKER: What are some of the differences between your day-to-day work on those courts and your current day-to-day work on the Supreme Court?

JUSTICE SOTOMAYOR: I've often described the difference between the three courts as follows. District court life is like controlled chaos. . . . The amount of information you absorb as a judge . . . , is so large that . . ., I told a friend that I finally understood why the brain is a muscle. All the knowledge I was stuffing into it, it's a good thing it was a muscle and could stretch. It is not only varied in the matters the district court judge is handling, and the issues that you're dealing with, but it's also varied in your human interactions with people. . . .

. . . Court of Appeals and Appellate Court, it's a different kind of justice. You're trying and dealing within the parameters [guidelines] set by the Supreme Court and the precedence [previous ruling] it's created and the precedence of your own circuit and looking for uniformity in that part of your world in the circuit. You're trying to find justice under the law, as it exists at that moment in that place, your circuit.

When you're on the Supreme Court, and their life is more contemplative, . . . There's less volume, but . . . every case, the Supreme Court takes is a Supreme court case. And what that means is . . .

. . . that it's an unsettled area of law. . . . They're harder cases. . . .

. . . we're not just looking at the case before us. . . . every time we announce a principle of law, . . . we are deciding not just that case . . . but the cases that come after it. So . . . it's not uncommon in the Supreme Court for a Supreme Court Justice to ask a litigant [person involved in lawsuit] if we follow your rules, isn't the natural outcome this other extreme?

. . . And those are, very much, the stark differences between the three courts.

1. Why does Justice Sotomayor write that the Supreme Court cases that announce new principles of law are so important?

2. How does a case before a District Court judge and a Supreme Court justice differ?

PRIMARY SOURCE

Supreme Court Case:
Taylor v. *Louisiana*, 1975

In the U.S. judiciary system, juries are selected to hear evidence and decide questions of fact. In this 1975 case, Billy Taylor was convicted by a jury of kidnapping. He appealed, arguing that his right to a fair trial by a jury was violated because no women served on the jury. The Constitution of the State of Louisiana did not allow women to serve on juries unless they had submitted a written request to serve. The State argued that women serve special roles in society that would be particularly disrupted by jury duty.

The case before the Supreme Court questioned whether the exclusion of women from jury duty violated the 6th and 14th Amendment right to an impartial jury trial and a federal law guaranteeing a fair cross section of the population for juries in federal courts.

Majority Opinion, Justice Byron White

The Louisiana jury selection system does not disqualify women from jury service, but, in operation, its . . . impact is that only a very few women, . . ., are called for jury service. . . .

. . . the Court has . . . declared that the American concept of the jury trial contemplates a jury drawn from a fair cross section of the community. . . . *[T]he jury should* "be large enough to promote group deliberation, free from outside attempts at intimidation, and to provide a fair possibility for obtaining a representative cross-section of the community." . . .

Community participation . . . is not only consistent with our democratic heritage, but is also critical to public confidence in the fairness of the criminal justice system. . . .

. . . if they [women] are systematically eliminated from jury panels, the Sixth Amendment's fair cross-section requirement cannot be satisfied.

The States are free to grant exemptions from jury service to individuals in case of special hardship or incapacity and to those engaged in particular occupations the uninterrupted performance of which is critical to the community's welfare. . . . A system excluding all women, however, is a wholly different matter. It is untenable [indefensible] to suggest these days that it would be a special hardship for each and every woman to perform jury service or that society cannot spare *any* women from their present duties.

---

1. Is there a difference between a jury of peers and a jury composed of a fair cross section of a community? Explain your view.

2. Associate Justice Rehnquist wrote a dissenting opinion, arguing that although outdated, Louisiana's jury system was not unconstitutional. "[Without] any suggestion that [Taylor's] trial was unfairly conducted, or that its result was unreliable, I would not require Louisiana to retry him. . . ." Do you agree or disagree with Rehnquist's argument?

PRIMARY SOURCE

Presidential Radio Talk: Supreme Court Justices
August 9, 1996

If given the opportunity to nominate a justice to the Supreme Court, a President puts a great deal of thought into this decision. The appointment is a lifetime position, and whoever is chosen will have a long-term impact on legal issues for the entire country. Not every candidate nominated by the President wins Senate approval, however. Considerations for nomination include the intellect, legal philosophy and previous decisions, leadership, background, temperament, political affiliation, and likelihood of being confirmed.

The following is an excerpt from a radio address that President Ronald Reagan gave related to his nominations of Justices William Rehnquist and Antonin Scalia.

The United States Senate began hearings on the nominations of William Rehnquist and Antonin Scalia, men I've named to the position of Chief Justice of the Supreme Court and Associate Justice of the Court. These hearings are a healthy process, mandated by our Constitution. . . . [T]hey provide the American people with an opportunity to evaluate for themselves the quality of a President's appointments.

. . . I was especially delighted with his nomination because Judge Scalia is the first Italian American in history to be named to the Supreme Court.

Beyond their undoubted legal qualifications, [they] embody a certain approach to the law—that as your President I consider it my duty to endorse. . . .

The background here is important. You see, during the last few election campaigns, one of the principal points I made to the American people was the need for a real change in the make-up of the Federal judiciary. I pointed out that too many judges were taking upon themselves the prerogatives [rights] of elected officials. Instead of interpreting the law according to the intent of the Constitution and the Congress, they were simply using the courts to strike down laws that displeased them politically or philosophically.

I argued the need for judges who would <u>interpret</u> law, not make it. The people, through their elected representatives, make our laws, and the people deserve to have these laws enforced as they were written.

Of course this upsets those who disagree with me politically—and I have a lurking suspicion that politics had more than a little to do with some of the tactics used against Justice Rehnquist. But I'm confident that mindful of their superb legal qualifications, the Senate will confirm [them] . . . And I can assure you: we will appoint more judges like them to the Federal bench. . . .

1. What approach to law did these men exhibit that Reagan espoused?

2. In what way does Reagan bring politics into the nominating process?

Lesson 1 The Unalienable Rights

CLOSE READING

A Commitment to Individual Rights

1. **Identify Key Steps in a Process** Describe the events that led to the adoption of the Bill of Rights. Explain how these events reflected a commitment to personal freedom.

2. **Compare and Contrast** Compare and contrast *civil liberties* and *civil rights*. What distinctions can be made between the two terms?

Limited Government

3. **Paraphrase** Read Justice Robert H. Jackson's opinion from *West Virginia Board of Education v. Barnette*, noted in this section. Paraphrase his statement.

4. **Explain an Argument** How does the following quotation by Justice Oliver Wendell Holmes from *Schenck* v. *United States* illustrate the concept that "rights are relative, not absolute"?

   "The most stringent protection of free speech would not protect a man in falsely shouting fire in a theatre and causing a panic."

   —*Schenck* v. *United States*, 1919

5. **Use Visual Information** Look at the image showing Japanese Americans being sent to incarceration camps during World War II. How does this image illustrate the issues that were involved in the forced evacuation of American citizens of Japanese descent? Discuss the reasons for and against this practice. Explain how our government responded years later.

The 14th Amendment, Fundamental Rights, and Federalism

6. **Summarize** Write a brief that applies to the 1925 *Gitlow* v. *New York* Supreme Court case. Include the following elements: statement of facts, statement of main issue, arguments, conclusion, and a summary of the case's significance.

7. **Compare and Contrast** As you read the text, use this graphic organizer to record your thoughts on the following questions: What are some of the characteristics of the 9th Amendment? What are some of the characteristics of the 14th Amendment? How are these two amendments similar?

The 9th Amendment and the 14th Amendment

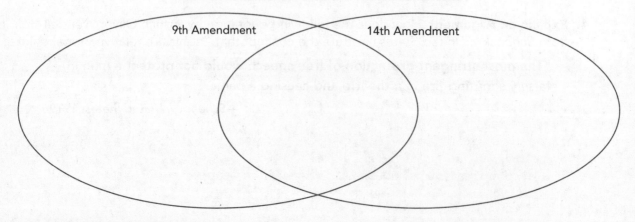

9th Amendment   14th Amendment

Lesson 2 Freedom of Religion

CLOSE READING

Religious Liberty

1. **Determine Central Ideas** As you read the lesson "Freedom of Religion," select and list the four cases that you think are the most significant regarding the protection of freedom of religion, and include a statement explaining why you think each case is significant.

2. **Draw Inferences** Consider Alexis de Tocqueville's quote from *Democracy in America,* noted in the first paragraph of the lesson. Explain what you think he meant when he wrote that it was not until he went into the churches that he "came to understand the genius and the power of this country."

Religion and Education

3. **Categorize** Categorize each of the following as "constitutional" or "unconstitutional" based on the criteria established in *Lemon* v. *Kurtzman.*
   A. a law that provides for reimbursements to private schools to cover their costs for teachers' salaries, textbooks, and other teaching materials in nonreligious courses
   B. the use of public funds to pay for field trips for parochial school students
   C. a law that provides for church-related schools to be reimbursed for the costs of administering State standardized tests
   D. the use of public funds to pay any part of the salaries of parochial school teachers who teach secular courses
   E. the use of public funds to provide an interpreter for a deaf student in a Catholic high school
   F. a law that creates a school district to benefit handicapped Jewish children

4. **Summarize** Consider released time programs, and summarize Supreme Court rulings on this issue.

Other Establishment Clause Cases

5. **Make Inferences** Consider the 1984 case of Pawtucket, Rhode Island in which the Court held that the city could include the Christian nativity scene in its holiday display. What question arose from this ruling, and what effect did it have on future rulings?

6. **Compare and Contrast** Consider the two public displays of the Ten Commandments referenced in the text. Which was allowed to remain partly because it is part of a larger display of historical and cultural markers? Which was ordered to be removed because it amounted to an endorsement of religion by government?

The Free Exercise Clause

7. **Identify Supporting Details** As you read the text "The Free Exercise Clause," use this graphic organizer to record information about how the Supreme Court has ruled on cases involving the Free Exercise Clause. Record limits the Court has placed on the free exercise of religion and examples of instances in which the Court has upheld the free exercise of religion.

Free Exercise Clause Cases	
Limits on Free Exercise	Free Exercise Upheld

Lesson 3 Freedom of Speech and Press

CLOSE READING

The Right of Free Expression

1. **Identify Central Issues** In what ways are the rights of free speech and press limited?

2. **Draw Conclusions** A citizen has written a letter to the editor of the local newspaper, accusing a local restaurant owner of adding fake charges to customers' bills. Can the restaurant owner sue? Why or why not?

Seditious Speech

3. **Compare and Contrast** Compare and contrast the interpretation of the Smith Act of 1940 in the cases of *Dennis* v. *U.S.* and *Yates* v. *U.S.*

The 1st Amendment and Symbolic Speech

4. **Summarize** The Supreme Court has made several rulings on acts of symbolic speech. Use the graphic organizer to identify at least six cases and how the Court ruled in each.

Supreme Court Rulings on Symbolic Speech

Supreme Court Case	Ruling

5. **Analyze Interactions** In the case *Tinker* v. *Des Moines,* the Court found that school officials had violated students' right to free expression. Furthermore, the Court emphasized that neither students nor teachers can be expected to "shed their constitutional rights to freedom of speech or expression at the schoolhouse gate." Yet, the Court has also endorsed the "comprehensive authority of school officials to prescribe and control conduct in the schools." How can these two positions coexist?

Prior Restraint on Expression

6. **Apply Concepts** A Nebraska State trial judge forbade all press coverage of a murder trial. In *Nebraska Press Association* v. *Stuart,* 1976, the Supreme Court held that the order was unconstitutional. What was the likely basis for this decision?

The Media in a Free Society

7. **Determine Central Ideas** In what way do shield laws limit government regulation of the media?

8. **Evaluate Arguments** The Court has established a three-part test to define obscenity, including applying "local community standards" in determining whether materials are offensive. How might the "local community" element of the test be affected when considering materials sent over the Internet?

Lesson 4 Freedom of Assembly and Petition

CLOSE READING

Constitutional Provisions

1. **Determine Central Ideas** Why is the right to assemble peaceably important to a democratic society?

2. **Cite Evidence** At what point does a constitutionally protected right to assemble become a case of civil disobedience? Cite evidence from the text to support your answer.

Time, Place, and Manner Rules

3. **Analyze Information** Complete the graphic organizer as you read this section. Then use it to answer these questions: On what basis can the government regulate assemblies? How do these parameters protect citizens' constitutional rights?

Case	Issue	Ruling
Grayned v. City of Rockford, 1972		
Cox v. Louisiana, 1965		
Coates v. Cincinnati, 1971		
Forsyth County v. Nationalist Movement, 1992		

Assemblies on Public and Private Property

4. **Compare and Contrast** Compare and contrast the Court's rulings regarding demonstrations in the cases of *Gregory* v. *Chicago*, 1969, and *Lloyd Corporation* v. *Tanner*, 1972. What was the basis for the Court's decisions in each case?

5. **Apply Concepts** Suppose you were part of a group demonstrating in front of city hall and you were arrested because the group had not given the city advance notice of the demonstration. Would your arrest be upheld by the Supreme Court? Explain your answer.

Freedom of Association

6. **Determine Central Ideas** How does the constitutional right of association extend the constitutional right of assembly?

7. **Evaluate Explanations** The Supreme Court has upheld the right of association as an "inseparable aspect" of the Constitution's guarantees of free expression. Moreover, it has held that there is no *absolute* right of association. Explain the differences between these two aspects of the right of association.

Lesson 5 Due Process of Law

CLOSE READING

Understanding Due Process

1. **Determine Central Ideas** The 5th Amendment declares that the Federal Government cannot deprive any person of "life, liberty, or property, without due process of law." The 14th Amendment places that same restriction on all State and local governments as well. Why is it important that the 14th Amendment places that same restriction on State and local governments?

2. **Draw Conclusions** Explain the logic behind the Supreme Court's unanimous decision in *Rochin* v. *California*, 1952, that the deputies in the case had violated the 14th Amendment's guarantee of procedural due process. What can you conclude from the fact that the decision was unanimous?

3. **Explain an Argument** Explain why the Supreme Court held that the Oregon compulsory school-attendance law, requiring all persons between the ages of eight and sixteen to attend public schools, violated the 14th Amendment's guarantee of substantive due process.

4. **Compare and Contrast** Use the Venn diagram to show how procedural due process and substantive due process are alike and different. Include a definition and an illustrative court case for each type of due process.

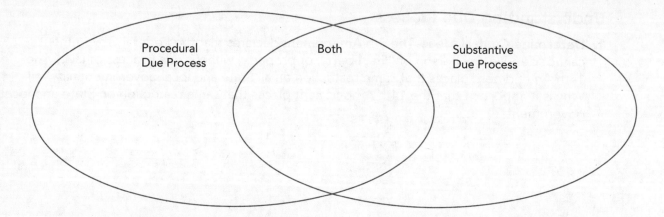

Individual Rights and the Public Good

5. **Integrate Information from Diverse Sources** Courts must often strike a balance between protecting public health, safety, morals, and general welfare and protecting individual freedoms. State and federal courts often decide in favor of the police power, however. Think of an example to demonstrate this fact, other than those found in the text.

6. **Assess an Argument** Eminent domain is the right of the government to take private property for public use; however, the government must provide the owners with just compensation. Consider the case of the building of the Interstate Highway System mentioned in the text. Do you agree with eminent domain in this case, and in general? Why or why not?

Lesson 6 Freedom and Security of the Person

CLOSE READING

Slavery and Involuntary Servitude

1. **Draw Inferences** The 13th Amendment forbids slavery and involuntary servitude anywhere within the United States. However, drafting young men into the military and forcing prisoners to work are legal. Why is this?

2. **Draw Conclusions** The Supreme Court ruled in favor of Jones in the case *Jones* v. *Mayer*, 1968, declaring that Congress has the power to abolish "the badges and incidents of slavery." How was Mayer's refusal to sell Jones a home considered a badge and incident of slavery?

Right to Keep and Bear Arms

3. **Paraphrase**. The 2nd Amendment reads: "A well regulated Militia, being necessary to the security of a free state, the right of the people to keep and bear Arms, shall not be infringed." What does this amendment mean to you in your own words? What has the Supreme Court said it means?

Security of Home and Person

4. **Cause and Effect** Why has the 3rd Amendment had little importance since 1791?

5. **Categorize** As you read "Security of Home and Person," place a check mark in the column labeled "Allowable" if evidence obtained through each method described can be used in court. If evidence obtained in this manner cannot be used in court, place a check mark in the column labeled "Not Allowable."

Security of Home and Person

Action	Allowable	Not Allowable
Evidence obtained in a home or on a person without a warrant		
Evidence obtained "in plain view"		
Evidence obtained via informational roadblocks		
Evidence obtained in a moving vehicle when there is probable cause to believe the vehicle is being used for illegal activities		

The Exclusionary Rule

6. **Explain an Argument** Provide one argument for and one argument against the exclusionary rule.

The Right of Privacy

7. **Draw Conclusions** What does the text mean when it says, "As the composition of the Court has changed . . . so has the Court's position on abortion."

8. **Identify** According to the Supreme Court's ruling in *Roe* v. *Wade*, at what point can the State legally prohibit abortion?

Lesson 7 Rights of the Accused

CLOSE READING

Article I Protections

1. **Determine Central Ideas** As you read this lesson, consider how the Constitution protects the rights of the accused. Complete the chart to show how the following features of the justice system protect the rights of the accused at different stages.

The Right of the Accused

Right	How the Right Protects the Accused
reading of Miranda rights	
writ of habeas corpus	
grand jury	
jury trial	
prohibition against cruel or unusual punishment	

Grand Jury and Double Jeopardy

2. **Evaluate Explanations** Do you agree with critics of the grand jury who say it is "too time consuming, too expensive, and too likely to follow the dictates of the prosecutor"? Why or why not? Give evidence from the text to support your answer.

Going to Trial

3. **Assess an Argument** If the 6th Amendment guarantees a public trial, why do some critics argue that media coverage jeopardizes a defendant's right to a fair trial?

Guarantee Against Self-Incrimination

4. Draw Conclusions Does the Miranda rule protect a suspect from being held in contempt of court? Explain your answer.

Bail and Preventive Detention

5. Analyze Information Would a standard fee for bail that is the same for every person accused of a crime be more or less fair than one set "in accordance with the severity of the crime charged and with the reputation and financial resources of the accused"? Explain your answer.

Cruel and Unusual Punishments

6. Identify Central Ideas The Supreme Court has excluded death by firing squad and by electric chair from the prohibition against cruel and unusual punishment. How does the Court justify this point of view?

Capital Punishment and Treason

7. Analyze Information Why have most recent capital punishment cases centered on "the application, not the constitutionality, of the punishment"?

8. Identify Supporting Details Why can treason only be committed during wartime?

PRIMARY SOURCE

Essay: "Civil Disobedience," Henry David Thoreau

Acts of civil disobedience have been around for centuries. However, the idea became more well known upon the publication of Henry David Thoreau's essay "On the Duty of Civil Disobedience." It was written following Thoreau's imprisonment for protesting against the government's support of slavery and the Mexican–American War. He was imprisoned after refusing to pay a poll tax. Thoreau felt that the war was a plan to expand slavery, and he did not want his tax dollars funding either policy. The essay reflects his conviction that it is not enough to disagree with injustice—one must act. Thoreau's ideas have inspired many others, including Martin Luther King, Jr.

Can there not be a government in which majorities do not virtually decide right and wrong, but conscience?—in which majorities decide only those questions to which the rule of expediency is applicable? Must the citizen ever for a moment, or in the least degree, resign his conscience to the legislator? Why has every man a conscience, then? I think that we should be men first, and subjects afterward. . . . Law never made men a whit [small amount] more just; and, by means of their respect for it, even the well-disposed are daily made the agents of injustice. . . .

How can a man be satisfied to entertain an opinion merely, and enjoy *it*? Is there any enjoyment in it, if his opinion is that he is aggrieved? . . . Action from principle,—the perception and the performance of right,—changes things and relations. . . .

Unjust laws exist: shall we be content to obey them, or shall we endeavor to amend them, and obey them until we have succeeded, or shall we transgress them at once? Men generally, under such a government as this, think that they ought to wait until they have persuaded the majority to alter them. They think that, if they should resist, the remedy would be worse than the evil. But it is the fault of the government itself that the remedy is worse than the evil. *It* makes it worse. Why is it not more apt to anticipate and provide for reform? . . . Why does it not encourage its citizens to be on the alert to point out its faults, and *do* better than it would have them? . . .

If the injustice has a spring, or a pulley, or a rope, or a crank, exclusively for itself, then perhaps you may consider whether the remedy will not be worse than the evil; but if it is of such a nature that it requires you to be the agent of injustice to another, then, I say, break the law. Let your life be a counter friction to stop the machine. What I have to do is to see, at any rate, that I do not lend myself to the wrong which I condemn.

1. Thoreau stacks his argument with rhetorical questions. What effect does this have on the reader?

2. According to Thoreau, what is the goal of resisting the government?

Supreme Court Case:
Lemon v. *Kurtzman*, 1971

The fact that the principle of separation of church and state was part of the 1st Amendment illustrates its importance to the Founders. Ensuring that there is a distinct "wall" between the two has been an ongoing challenge, however. Often, the Supreme Court has had to play a major role in determining how to keep the church and state separate, especially in education. In 1971, two cases were brought to the Court under the umbrella of *Lemon* v. *Kurtzman*. In an 8-1 decision, both cases were found to be unconstitutional. The laws that were found to be unconstitutional allowed the State to reimburse or pay private religious schools for the salaries of the teachers who taught there and/or for the cost of textbooks.

Majority Opinion, Chief Justice Warren E. Burger

In *Allen* the Court refused to make assumptions . . . about the religious content of the textbooks that the State would be asked to provide. We cannot, however, refuse here to recognize that teachers have a substantially different ideological character from books. In terms of potential for involving some aspect of faith or morals in secular [nonreligious] subjects, a textbook's content is ascertainable, but a teacher's handling of a subject is not. . . .

The schools are governed by the standards set forth in a 'Handbook of School Regulations'. . . . It emphasizes the role and importance of the teacher in parochial schools: "The prime factor for the success or the failure of the school is the spirit and personality, as well as the professional competency, of the teacher". . . . [and] that: 'Religious formation is not confined to formal courses; nor is it restricted to a single subject area.'. . .

We need not and do not assume that teachers in parochial schools will be guilty of bad faith or any conscious design to evade the limitations imposed by the statute and the First Amendment. We simply recognize that a dedicated religious person, teaching in a school affiliated with his or her faith and operated to inculcate [teach] its tenets [principles], will inevitably experience great difficulty in remaining religiously neutral. . . .

We do not assume, however, that parochial school teachers will be unsuccessful in their attempts to segregate their religious beliefs from their secular educational responsibilities. But the potential for impermissible fostering of religion is present. The Rhode Island Legislature has not, and could not, provide state aid on the basis of a mere assumption that secular teachers under religious discipline can avoid conflicts. The State must be certain, given the Religion Clauses, that subsidized teachers do not inculcate [teach] religion. . . .

Dissenting Opinion, Justice Byron White

The Court strikes down the Rhode Island statute on its face. No fault is found with the secular purpose of the program; there is no suggestion that the purpose of the program was aid to religion disguised in secular attire. Nor does the Court find that the primary effect of the program is to aid religion rather than to implement secular goals. The Court nevertheless finds that impermissible "entanglement" will result from administration of the program. The reasoning is a curious and mystifying blend, but a critical factor appears to be an unwillingness to accept the District Court's express findings that on the evidence before it none of the teachers here involved mixed religious and secular instruction. . . .

Accepting the District Court's observation in *DiCenso* that education is an integral part of the religious mission of the Catholic church. . . , the majority then interposes findings and conclusions that the District Court expressly abjured [rejected], namely, that nuns, clerics, and dedicated Catholic laymen unavoidably pose a grave risk in that they might not be able to put aside their religion in the secular classroom. Although stopping short of considering them untrustworthy, the Court concludes that for them the difficulties of avoiding teaching religion along with secular subjects would pose intolerable risks and would in any event entail an unacceptable enforcement regime. Thus, the potential for impermissible fostering of religion in secular classrooms. . . .

The Court thus creates an insoluble paradox for the State and the parochial schools. The State cannot finance secular instruction if it permits religion to be taught in the same classroom; but if it exacts a promise that religion not be so taught—a promise the school and its teachers are quite willing and on this record able to give—and enforces it, it is then entangled in the "no entanglement" aspect of the Court's Establishment Clause jurisprudence.

---

1. What is the central argument that Chief Justice Warren uses against the Rhode Island case?

2. What is Justice White's main criticism of the majority opinion?

3. Of the three-pronged standard that was developed in *Lemon*, the Rhode Island case failed the "excessive entanglement" portion of the standard. Why did it fail?

Lesson 1 American Citizenship

CLOSE READING

Citizenship in the United States

1. **Explain an Argument** Should U.S. citizenship be considered a right or a privilege?

Natural-Born Citizens

2. **Summarize** As you read "Natural-Born Citizens," use this graphic organizer to record details of the two ways of acquiring citizenship by birth: jus soli and jus sanguinis.

Jus Soli	Jus Sanguinis

Naturalized Citizens

3. **Explain an Argument** Should citizens by birth have to meet the same requirements as those set for naturalized citizens?

Losing One's Citizenship

4. Compare and Contrast Compare and contrast expatriation and denaturalization.

Government Immigration Policies

5. Determine Central Ideas How has U.S. immigration policy changed over time?

6. Identify Supporting Details What groups of people are presently excluded from entering the United States?

Policies on Unauthorized Immigrants

7. Cite Evidence With what current immigration issues does the United States have to deal?

8. Integrate Information from Diverse Sources Read the last paragraph of "Policies on Unauthorized Immigrants." Then look at the political cartoon. Do the text and the cartoon both tell you the same information concerning immigration reform?

Lesson 2 Diversity and Discrimination

CLOSE READING

A Changing American Culture

1. **Identify Cause and Effect** Explain the impact that immigration policies can have on the heterogeneous nature of the United States.

Discrimination in America

2. **Assess an Argument** Read this statement by Supreme Court Justice John Marshall Harlan, dissenting in *Plessy* v. *Ferguson*, 1896:

   "Our Constitution is color-blind, and neither knows nor tolerates classes among citizens. In respect of civil rights, all citizens are equal before the law. The humblest is the peer of the most powerful."

   Taking the perspective of one of the minority groups you have read about that has suffered race-based discrimination in the United States, respond to Harlan's comment. Do you believe that what he says is true? Explain, giving examples.

3. **Compare and Contrast** Study the information provided below. Choose two of the groups to compare and contrast in terms of the discrimination they have experienced. Organize your ideas as a comparison-contrast paragraph.

African Americans	Native Americans	Hispanic Americans	Asian Americans
• slavery • push for civil rights • continued discrimination every day	• driven from lands • forced relocation to reservations • poverty, joblessness, and health issues such as, shorter lifespan	• voter restrictions and labor discrimination • deportations • anti-immigrant viewpoints directed at larger Hispanic American groups	• workplace violence • Chinese Exclusion Act • World War II relocation camps

4. **Draw Inferences** How might differences in language, religion, and culture within an ethnic group cause problems as that group tries to obtain equal rights?

Discrimination Against Women

5. **Identify Supporting Details** Efforts to promote women's equality in the United States began in 1848. In 2009, with the Lily Ledbetter Fair Pay Act, Congress took action to try to ensure fair pay for women. What evidence is there that more efforts are still necessary?

6. **Draw Inferences** Why is on-the-job discrimination the most readily identifiable form of discrimination against women?

Lesson 3 Equality Before the Law

CLOSE READING

Equal Protection and Individual Rights

1. **Summarize** Review the paragraph that quotes the 14th Amendment's Equal Protection Clause. What does it mean to say that all people must receive the *equal protection* of the laws?

2. **Draw Inferences** Reread the section about strict scrutiny. Give an example of a situation in which it is reasonable to discriminate against a class of people.

A History of Segregation

3. **Explain an Argument** How did the case of *Plessy* v. *Ferguson* undermine the Equal Protection Clause?

4. **Analyze Sequence** Review the text on *Brown* v. *Board of Education*. Make a list of cases that led up to *Brown* v. *Board of Education*. How did each case pave the way for the decision in *Brown*? What is the overall trend established by these cases?

5. **Identify Cause and Effect** How can de facto segregation come about without laws that require it?

Gender, Sexual Orientation, and Equality

6. **Assess an Argument** Study the photo that shows male and female students at West Point, and consider what had to happen to get them there. How did equal protection cases dealing with race provide a precedent for cases involving sex discrimination?

7. **Evaluate Explanations** Why do you think the Court has not held *all* sex-based discrimination to be unconstitutional?

8. **Analyze Interactions** What is the connection between the Court's ruling on the Defense of Marriage Act and its decisions in key civil rights cases, such as *Brown* v. *Board of Education*?

Lesson 4 Federal Civil Rights Laws

CLOSE READING

The History of Civil Rights Laws

1. **Determine Author's Purpose** Study the photo of Dr. Martin Luther King, Jr., again and consider how his actions affected the society around him. What did Dr. King mean when he commented that "Judicial decrees may not change the heart, but they can restrain the heartless"?

2. **Draw Conclusions** Explain how the Serviceman's Readjustment Act of 1944 (the GI Bill of Rights) made a difference to minority groups.

3. **Compare and Contrast** Review the section of text about the Civil Rights Acts of 1964 and 1968. How did each law affect civil rights overall?

4. **Analyze Interactions** Consider the section in the text about Title IX of the Education Amendments of 1972. How would you expect this legislation to affect women economically?

Government Policies on Affirmative Action

5. **Compare and Contrast** Review the table in the text titled "Two Views on Affirmative Action." List the key arguments made by each view in the graphic organizer below, then answer the following question: Which viewpoint is more compelling to you, and why?

Louis Menand, "The Changing Meaning of Affirmative Action"	Artemus Ward, "Is Affirmative Action Justified?"

6. **Assess an Argument** Look at the photo of Allan Bakke again, and reread its caption. Supreme Court Justice Sandra Day O'Connor wrote, "The Constitution protects persons, not groups. Whenever the government treats any person unequally because of his or her race, that person has suffered an injury." How do Justice O'Connor's words apply to reverse discrimination?

7. **Analyze Sequence** Reread the section of the text about affirmative action cases after *Bakke*. List three major cases in which the Supreme Court has ruled on affirmative action, from 1978 to the present, and explain the overall trend of these cases.

PRIMARY SOURCE

Supreme Court Case:
Ledbetter v. Goodyear Tire & Rubber Company, Inc., 2007

In 1998, Lilly Ledbetter filed a complaint of wage discrimination against Goodyear Tire and Rubber Company, where she had worked for almost 20 years. She claimed that she had been given poor evaluations because of her sex and her pay had not increased as it would have if she had been rated fairly. As a result, she earned much less than her male coworkers.

Lilly Ledbetter's fight for equal pay for equal work eventually involved all three branches of government, resulting in a law with her name on it: the Lilly Ledbetter Fair Pay Act of 2009.

Majority Opinion, Justice Samuel Alito

Title VII of the Civil Rights Act of 1964 makes it an "unlawful employment practice" to discriminate "against any individual with respect to his compensation . . . because of such individual's . . . sex." . . . An individual wishing to challenge an employment practice . . . must first file a charge with the EEOC [Equal Employment Opportunity Commission]. Such a charge must be filed within a specified period (either 180 or 300 days, depending on the State) "after the alleged unlawful employment practice occurred," . . . if the employee does not submit a timely EEOC charge, the employee may not [sue] in court.

Ledbetter should have filed an EEOC charge within 180 days after each allegedly discriminatory pay decision was made and communicated to her. She did not do so . . .

The EEOC filing deadline "protect[s] employers from the burden of defending claims arising from employment decisions that are long past."

. . . [T]he critical issue in [such a case] will often be whether the evaluation was so far off the mark that a sufficient inference of discriminatory intent can be drawn. . . . This can be a subtle determination, and the passage of time may seriously diminish the ability of the parties and the fact finder to reconstruct what actually happened.

Ledbetter, finally, makes a variety of policy arguments in favor of giving the alleged victims of pay discrimination more time before they are required to file a charge with the EEOC. Among other things, she claims that pay discrimination is harder to detect than other forms of employment discrimination.

We are not in a position to evaluate Ledbetter's policy arguments . . .

. . . We apply the statute as written, and this means that any unlawful employment practice, including those involving compensation, must be presented to the EEOC within the period prescribed by statute.

1. Why did Title VII put a time limit on filing complaints to the EEOC?

2. Is this decision an example of judicial restraint or judicial activism? Explain your reasoning.

Political Cartoon: Immigration by Mike Turner

Immigration has been a defining, often contentious, element throughout United States history. Immigrants from around the world have contributed to the American economy, culture, and politics. But at the same time, immigration has also been a source of furious debate and divisiveness. Anxiety over national security, economic and religious challenges, and a host of other factors have made immigration policy a central issue of politics.

"Immigrants...there goes the neighbourhood!"

1. What point is the cartoonist making in his drawing?

2. How can you tell how the Native Americans felt?

3. What can you infer about American attitudes regarding immigration to the U.S. from this cartoon?

PRIMARY SOURCE

Poem: "I, Too," Langston Hughes

Langston Hughes was a leading voice of the Harlem Renaissance, a significant cultural movement of Black intellectual, literary, and artistic life in the 1920s. This poem was written in 1926, as people of color struggled for social and economic equality. His writing reflected Black protest against racial injustice and raised questions about their place in a democratic nation.

I, too, sing America.

I am the darker brother.
They send me to eat in the kitchen
When company comes,
But I laugh,
And eat well,
And grow strong.

Tomorrow,
I'll be at the table
When company comes.
Nobody'll dare
Say to me,
"Eat in the kitchen,"
Then.

Besides,
They'll see how beautiful I am
And be ashamed—

I, too, am America.

1. Who are the "they" in the poem?

2. How does the poem show diversity and unity at the same time?

Lesson 1 The History of Voting Rights

CLOSE READING

Voting Rights in the United States

1. **Draw Inferences** How have candidates for office had to broaden their campaign messages from the early days of the republic to today?

2. **Summarize** Complete the chart to show how the American electorate has grown from the early days of our nation to the present. The first stage of expansion has been completed for you.

Stage	Dates	How Did The American Electorate Grow?
First	Early 1800s	Religious qualifications eliminated
Second		
Third		
Fourth		
Fifth		

The 15th Amendment

3. **Identify Cause and Effect** The 15th Amendment was ratified in 1870. It was intended to ensure that all African American men could vote. However, Congress did not take any action to enforce the new amendment. What impact did this have on African Americans for the next 90 years?

4. Draw Conclusions Why was using the courts to enforce the 15th Amendment not an ideal approach?

Civil Rights Acts of 1957, 1960, and 1964

5. Compare and Contrast How did enforcing the 15th Amendment through the Civil Rights Act of 1957 differ from the approach of taking cases to the Supreme Court?

6. Summarize Summarize the provisions of the Civil Rights Act of 1964.

Voting Rights Act of 1965—Then and Now

7. Cite Evidence Why has it been important to continue to amend the Voting Rights Act? Cite evidence from the text to support your answer.

8. Assess an Argument What was the Supreme Court's decision in *Shelby* v. *Holder*, 2013?

Lesson 2 Your Right to Vote

CLOSE READING

Voting Qualifications and the Federal Government

1. **Summarize** Briefly describe who is allowed to vote in this country, based on the five constitutional restrictions on a State's ability to set suffrage qualifications.

2. **Apply Concepts** Beyond the five restrictions you have read about, no State can violate provisions in the Constitution regarding suffrage qualifications. Give an example of a suffrage qualification that would violate a constitutional provision.

Universal Criteria for Voting

3. **Summarize** What are the criteria for voting in the United States, and how have they changed over time? As you read "Universal Criteria for Voting," use this graphic organizer to record information about past and current voter qualifications in the United States.

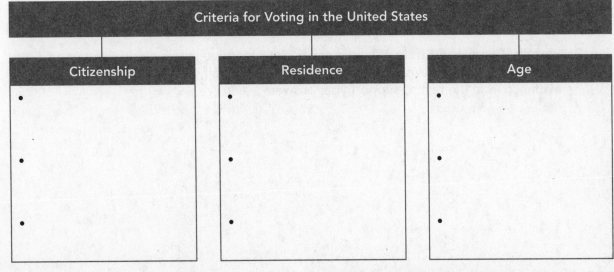

Criteria for Voting in the United States

Citizenship	Residence	Age
•	•	•
•	•	•
•	•	•

4. **Draw Conclusions** Why do you suppose that more voters who are 65 or older vote in elections than do voters in the 18- to 20-year-old age range?

The Voter Registration Process

5. **Vocabulary: Use Context Clues** Read the first paragraph of the text "The Voter Registration Process." What does the word *fraudulent* mean in this paragraph? Do you think voter registration helps election officials prevent fraudulent voting? Why or why not?

6. **Assess an Argument** Read about the controversies surrounding the voter registration process. Consider the views of both critics and proponents of current registration requirements. What can you conclude about voter registration requirements based on the views of both sides?

Historical Criteria for Voting

7. **Identify Cause and Effect** Why did some States enforce literacy requirements as a condition for voting? What caused Congress to eventually ban these requirements? Use evidence from the text to support your answer.

Lesson 3 Voting Trends

CLOSE READING

Voter Turnout in the United States

1. **Draw Inferences** Now that you have learned about the origins of the word *idiot*, what can you infer about Greek attitudes toward participating in public life?

2. **Draw Conclusions** What is meant by "off-year elections"? Compare voter turnout in off-year elections to elections in other years.

Why People Do Not Vote

3. **Determine Central Ideas** Why is it true that several million persons who are regularly identified as nonvoters can be more accurately described as "cannot-voters"?

4. **Assess an Argument** What reasons do voters give to defend their decision not to go to the polls?

Influences on Voters and Voting Behavior

5. **Draw Inferences** What are some ways in which the study of voting behavior can impact future elections and the election process?

Sociological Factors and Political Attitudes

6. Summarize Complete the chart with one example showing how each sociological factor historically has affected voting.

Sociological Factors Affecting Voting

Sociological Factor	Example of Effect on Voting
Income	
Occupation	
Education	
Gender	
Age	
Religion	
Ethnic Background	
Geography	

Psychological Factors and Political Attitudes

7. Compare and Contrast What are some arguments for and against voting according to party loyalty? What are some arguments for and against voting independently and considering how each candidate, regardless of party, handles the important issues?

8. Apply Concepts The impression a candidate makes on the voters can greatly help or hurt them. How do you think candidates should present themselves to win your vote?

Lesson 4 The Voting Process

CLOSE READING

Filling Elected Public Offices

1. **Cite Evidence** The Help America Vote Act of 2002 has had a significant impact on the electoral process. What is this act, and what impact is it intended to have on voters' rights and election outcomes? Use evidence from the text to support your answer.

Precincts, Polling Places, and Ballots

2. **Analyze Interactions** Several different groups and individuals manage the local voting process. Identify these officials and their roles.

3. **Summarize** The text describes how voting in the United States has moved from voice voting to unofficial paper ballots to official secret ballots. Drawing on evidence from the text, summarize the reasons for these changes.

4. **Draw Conclusions** To what degree did political "machines" have a significant impact on election results? Draw on the text to answer this question.

5. **Draw Inferences** How do political parties expect voters to make use of a sample ballot?

Casting and Counting Ballots

6. **Determine Central Ideas** Various methods of electronic voting and vote counting have been tried over the years. What drawback(s) do all of these methods have in common?

7. **Summarize** Describe the steps in the process of voting by mail.

8. **Assess an Argument** Complete the chart to show the pros and cons of three ways of voting that might be in your future: in-person voting at polling places, mail-in voting, and Internet voting. After you complete the chart, write a sentence telling which way, or ways, you think voters should be allowed to cast their ballots in the future.

Voting Options	Pros	Cons
In-person voting at polling places		
Mail-in voting		
Online voting		

Lesson 5 Public Opinion and Polling

CLOSE READING

What Is Public Opinion?

1. **Determine Meaning of Words** As you read "What Is Public Opinion?" pay particular attention to the term *publics*. What is meant by this term? How do you think the idea of multiple "publics" affects the process of understanding public opinion? Use evidence from the text to support your answer.

Family, School, and Political Attitudes

2. **Identify Cause and Effect** As you read "Family, School, and Political Attitudes," use this graphic organizer to list four ways that family and school can influence political attitudes and the effect of each on children.

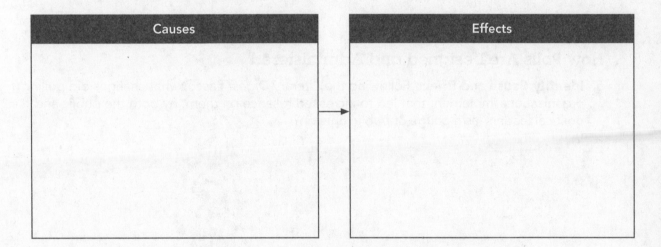

Causes	Effects

Other Factors That Influence Political Attitudes and Actions

3. **Draw Conclusions** The text describes how historic events, such as the Great Depression and the Vietnam War, have shaped Americans' political opinions. How do you think events of the last decade—for example, changes in economic conditions and communication technology—have changed Americans' political opinions?

Ways to Measure Public Opinion

4. Analyze Word Choices The author says that "the media are frequently said to be 'mirrors' as well as 'molders' of opinion." What do the words *mirrors* and *molders* mean in this context? Cite evidence from the text to support your answer.

Public Opinion Polls

5. Cite Evidence Certain types of public opinion polls are particularly susceptible to error. Cite evidence from this text to identify which types, explain why this is the case, and describe how pollsters have worked to overcome these issues.

How Polls Are Designed and Administered

6. Identify Cause and Effect Following the *Literary Digest* fiasco, what changes did polling organizations implement that led to increased reliance on them, by both the public and political leaders, as a gauge of public opinion?

Poll Reliability

7. Make Generalizations How much should voters be swayed by the results of public opinion polls when deciding how to cast their ballots? Why?

Lesson 6 Influencing Public Opinion: The Mass Media

CLOSE READING

The Role of Mass Media

1. **Identify Key Steps in a Process** Use this flowchart to record the development of different mass media over time.

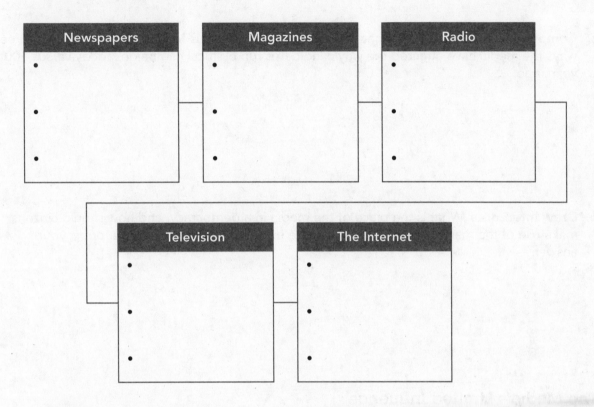

2. **Compare and Contrast** How did the advent of television change how candidates ran their political campaigns? Similarly, how has the advent of the Internet changed how candidates run their campaigns today?

3. **Integrate Information from Diverse Sources** Barack Obama's use of the Internet and social media in both the 2008 and 2012 campaigns has been hailed as a key tool in his successful presidential campaigns. Based on what you have read about the history of the Internet, your personal experiences with the Internet, and any knowledge you have of the Obama campaign, or other campaigns, what Internet strategies do you think are especially effective in political campaigns?

How the Media Affects Politics

4. **Support Ideas with Examples** Explain the media's role in shaping the public agenda. Use a contemporary or historical issue with which you are familiar as an example to support your reasoning.

5. **Compare and Contrast** Use what you have learned from this text to describe at least three ways the media have affected the way candidates run political campaigns today versus 100 years ago.

6. **Draw Inferences** What is the place of the media in a democracy, and how should citizens make use of the media available to them? Use evidence from the text to support your answer.

The Media's Limited Influence

7. **Identify Cause and Effect** This reading notes that most people are more interested in being entertained than informed. What are some of the effects of this attitude on television programming? Use evidence from the text to support your answer.

8. **Cite Evidence** In what way is an article on new fishing conservation efforts in *Field & Stream* magazine an example of how the media's influence is sometimes limited? Cite evidence from "The Media's Limited Influence" to support your answer.

Lesson 7 Understanding Interest Groups

CLOSE READING

What Are Interest Groups?

1. **Summarize** Summarize public attitudes toward interest groups, and describe their general role in the American political system.

Origins and Viewpoints

2. **Determine Author's Point of View** Read the following passage from James Madison's *The Federalist* No. 10, keeping in mind that he uses the word *faction* in place of the term *interest group*:

   "It could never be more truly said than of the first remedy that it was worse than the disease. Liberty is to faction what air is to fire, an ailment without which it instantly expires. But it could not be less folly to abolish liberty, which is essential to political life, because it nourishes faction, than it would be to wish the annihilation of air, which is essential to animal life, because it imparts to fire its destructive agency."

   Based on Madison's words, how do you think he feels about factions or interest groups?

3. **Identify Supporting Details** As you read, use this graphic organizer to record the positive and negative aspects of interest groups.

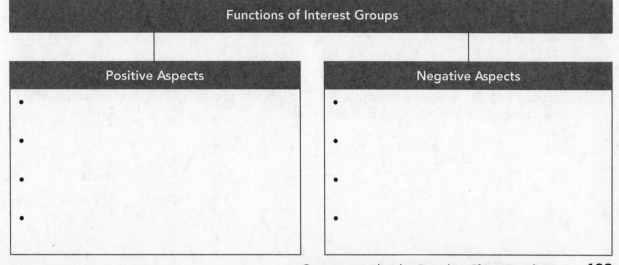

Functions of Interest Groups	
Positive Aspects	**Negative Aspects**
•	•
•	•
•	•
•	•

Why Do Individuals Join Interest Groups?

4. **Summarize** Summarize three reasons why interest groups grew in number in the 1960s and 1970s.

Processes Used By Interest Groups—The Direct Approach

5. **Identify Supporting Details** Identify at least one way in which lobbyists seek to influence each branch of government.

6. **Identify Cause and Effect** Detail the effects of the Abramoff scandal on subsequent lobbyists, including current lobbyists working in Washington, D.C. Use information from the text in your response.

Processes Used By Interest Groups—The Indirect Approach

7. **Summarize** Summarize four ways in which interest groups work indirectly to influence government and public opinion.

8. **Determine Central Issues** Using celebrity spokespeople is a common way for interest groups to try to influence policymakers. Do interest groups gain undue influence when celebrities back their causes? Explain.

PRIMARY SOURCE

Speech: The President and the Press: Address Before the American Newspaper Publishers Association, April 27, 1961

In the height of the Cold War, during President Kennedy's administration, the United States supported Cuban exiles in their attempt to overthrow Fidel Castro, whose government was becoming increasingly undemocratic. The invasion was a failure, in part because information was leaked by indiscreet intelligence talk that was published in newspapers.

In this address to the American Society of Newspaper Editors, President Kennedy appealed to editors to consider the impact on national security before publishing a story.

> . . . I do ask every publisher, every editor, and every newsman in the nation to reexamine his own standards, and to recognize the nature of our country's peril. In time of war, the government and the press have customarily joined in an effort based largely on self-discipline, to prevent unauthorized disclosures to the enemy. In time of "clear and present danger," the courts have held that even the privileged rights of the First Amendment must yield to the public's need for national security.
>
> If the press is awaiting a declaration of war before it imposes the self-discipline of combat conditions, then I can only say that no war ever posed a greater threat to our security. If you are awaiting a finding of "clear and present danger," then I can only say that the danger has never been more clear and its presence has never been more imminent.
>
> For the facts of the matter are that this nation's foes have openly boasted of acquiring through our newspapers information they would otherwise hire agents to acquire through theft, bribery or espionage. . . .
>
> I have no intention of establishing a new Office of War Information to govern the flow of news. I am not suggesting any new forms of censorship or any new types of security classifications. . . . But I am asking the members of the newspaper profession and the industry in this country to reexamine their own responsibilities, . . . and to heed the duty of self-restraint which that danger imposes upon us all.
>
> Every newspaper now asks itself, with respect to every story: "Is it news?" All I suggest is that you add the question: "Is it in the interest of the national security?"

1. What impact do you think this speech had on a free press?

2. Is President Kennedy infringing on the 1st Amendment in this request?

PRIMARY SOURCE

Supreme Court Case:
Brnovich v. Democratic National Committee, 2021

In this case, two Arizona voting laws were challenged as racially discriminating. One regulation required voters to cast their ballots in their assigned district. A vote cast outside the district was discarded. A second regulation involved mail-in ballots. These could be collected only by a family member, caregiver, or mail carrier.

The Voting Rights Act of 1965 (VRA) was enacted to prevent practices that suppressed the voting rights of people of color. The Democratic National Committee challenged Arizona's laws as too restrictive and in violation the VRA.

Majority Opinion, Justice Samuel Alito

. . . [E]very voting rule imposes a burden of some sort. Voting takes time and, for almost everyone, some travel, even if only to a nearby mailbox. Casting a vote . . . requires compliance with certain rules. But because voting necessarily requires some effort and compliance with some rules, the concept of a voting system that is "equally open" and that furnishes an equal "opportunity" to cast a ballot must tolerate the "usual burdens of voting." . . . Mere inconvenience cannot be enough to demonstrate a violation [of the VRA]. . . .

. . . [T]he mere fact that there is some disparity [inequality] in impact does not necessarily mean that a system is not equally open or that it does not give everyone an equal opportunity to vote. The size of any disparity matters. . . . very small differences should not be artificially magnified. . . .

. . . [I]t is important to consider the reason for the rule. Rules that are supported by strong state interests are less likely to violate [the VRA].

One strong and entirely legitimate state interest is the prevention of fraud. . . .

In light of the principles set out above, neither Arizona's out-of-precinct rule nor its ballot-collection law violates . . . the VRA. . . . Having to identify one's own polling place and then travel there to vote does not exceed the "usual burdens of voting."

. . . The plaintiffs were unable to provide statistical evidence showing that [Arizona's collection law] had a disparate impact on minority voters.

Limiting the classes of persons who may handle early ballots to those less likely to have ulterior motives deters potential fraud and improves voter confidence.

1. According to this decision, is it legal for laws to have a different impact on different groups of voters?

2. Why would statistical evidence be needed to show violation of the VRA?

PRIMARY SOURCE

Political Cartoon: Voter Turnout by Walt Handelsman

There are a variety of factors that affect voter turnout. The type of election matters. Low voting counts are most often seen in primary and local elections. Competitiveness of the races and the nature of the issues affect the number of voters going to the polls as well. Voter registration laws, voter identification laws, early voting, and ease of access to polling places all impact the voter participation.

Political cartoons can convey an artist's view of elections and reasons for how, why, and whether people cast their ballots. Such cartoons have an important role in the political arena, shaping conversations and informing the public about issues.

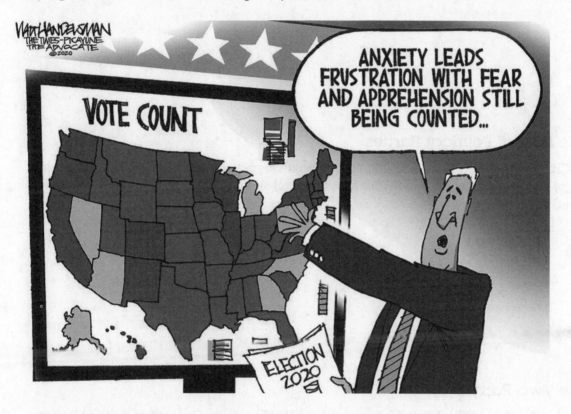

1. What emotional attributes does the announcer give the voters?

2. What point is the cartoonist making?

Lesson 1 Political Parties and What They Do

CLOSE READING

What Is a Political Party?

1. **Categorize** Describe the three separate, but closely related, elements that compose the two major American political parties.

The Role of Political Parties

2. **Cite Evidence** Provide an example of a political party performing the following roles: **(a)** nominating, **(b)** informing and activating, **(c)** serving as a bonding agent, **(d)** governing, **(e)** serving as a watchdog.

The Two-Party System

3. **Identify Supporting Details** As you read "The Two-Party System" and the following two texts, use this graphic organizer to record details about major and minor parties.

Identifying Supporting Details	
Major Parties	Minor Parties

Multiparty and One-Party Politics

4. **Compare and Contrast** Compare and contrast two-party with multiparty systems, noting the strengths and weaknesses of each.

Third and Minor Parties in the United States

5. **Draw Inferences** What type of minor party is likely to develop around the following: **(a)** a strong personality, **(b)** the collapse of the stock market, **(c)** a specific theory about government, **(d)** growing concern about climate change?

The Decentralized Nature of the Parties

6. **Determine Central Ideas** What does it mean to say that the major parties in American politics are decentralized? Would a more centralized political party be more or less effective at winning elections?

National Party Functions

7. **Analyze Interactions** Between presidential elections, what does the national committee of each party do?

State and Local Party Functions

8. **Draw Conclusions** How does party organization contribute to the strength of the two-party system?

Lesson 2 Nominations

CLOSE READING

Nominations: A Critical First Step

1. **Cite Evidence** Read "Impact of the Nominating Process." According to the text, how does the nominating process impact the right to vote in the United States?

2. **Cite Evidence** Read the second paragraph of "Methods of Nomination." According to the text, how do dictatorial regimes impact voting?

The Caucus

3. **Identify Supporting Details** Read the quote from *The Works of John Adams* (1856) describing the original caucus. How could this quote be used to support the criticisms of the original caucus?

The Convention

4. **Summarize** Briefly describe how conventions worked at the local, State, and national levels of government.

The Direct Primary

5. Compare and Contrast Read "The Closed Primary" and "The Open Primary." Compare and contrast these two forms of the direct primary using the Venn diagram below.

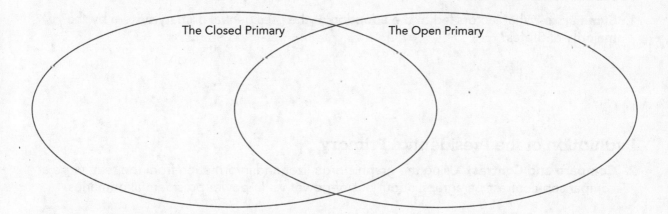

The Closed Primary   The Open Primary

6. Analyze Interactions Read "Versions of the Open Primary." How did California and Washington respond to the Supreme Court's decision in *California Democratic Party* v. *Jones*? How did Louisiana respond?

Evaluation of the Primary

7. Draw Conclusions Read the first paragraph of "Other Problems with the Primary." How can the direct primary have an effect on the party itself? Can you think of an example for this?

Petition

8. Infer How is filling an appointed office different from filling an elected office?

Lesson 3 Electing the President

CLOSE READING

Presidential Primaries

1. **Summarize** What factors led to the adoption of the presidential primary system by the majority of States?

Evaluation of the Presidential Primary

2. **Compare and Contrast** Using the graphic organizer and information from the text, write a comparison-contrast paragraph about out-of-power vs. in-power presidential primaries.

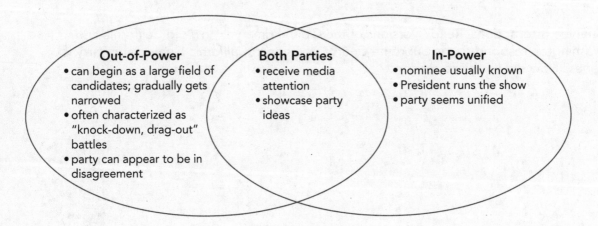

Out-of-Power
- can begin as a large field of candidates; gradually gets narrowed
- often characterized as "knock-down, drag-out" battles
- party can appear to be in disagreement

Both Parties
- receive media attention
- showcase party ideas

In-Power
- nominee usually known
- President runs the show
- party seems unified

The National Convention

3. **Analyze Sequence** Explain why both parties follow the same sequence of events at a national convention.

Who Is Nominated?

4. **Draw Conclusions** What career path is a good choice for someone who wants to be elected President one day? Why?

The Presidential Campaign

5. Paraphrase Suppose you are a voter living in a battleground State. In your own words, describe what you should expect to experience during a presidential campaign.

The Electoral College

6. Determine Central Ideas Barring any unusual circumstances, describe the typical outcome of the electoral college during an election.

Electoral College Scenarios

7. Draw Conclusions When partisan politics are prevalent, what are some issues involved in throwing a presidential election to the House of Representatives?

Proposed Reforms and a Defense

8. Explain an Argument What evidence do the defenders of the electoral college give to support their claim that fears about the system are exaggerated?

Lesson 4 Money and Elections

CLOSE READING

The Price of an Election

1. **Determine Central Ideas** Read "The Price of an Election." How could getting and spending campaign funds *corrupt* the political process?

Where the Money Comes From

2. **Identify Supporting Details** How do politicians pay for political campaigns? Who provides the money to pay for campaign expenses?

3. **Analyze Interactions** How does supporting campaigns with public money, in the form of government subsidies, support the political process in a democracy?

Federal Finance Laws

4. **Draw Inferences** What do you think President Obama meant when he commented that the *Citizens United* case might "open the floodgates for special interests"?

FEC Requirements

5. Draw Conclusions How does the Federal Election Commission (FEC) protect the political process from corruption by special interests?

6. Compare and Contrast How are contributions by political action committees (PACs) qualitatively different from contributions by individuals?

Loopholes in Finance Laws

7. Assess an Argument Do you agree with Senators John McCain and Russ Feingold that the use of soft money to finance campaigns should be limited? Why or why not?

8. Analyze Sequence Did the Supreme Court's ruling in the *Citizens United* case affect campaign spending in 2012? Explain.

PRIMARY SOURCE

CHARTS: Opinion Polls on Political Parties

Although there are dozens of political parties in the United States, American politics is dominated by the Democrats and Republicans—a two-party system. Yet many Americans do not feel as though their views are completely represented by either party. Over the years, Gallup has conducted polls about the need for a third party in American politics. The charts below reflect the data Gallup gathered when they asked Americans: In your view, do the Republican and Democratic parties do an adequate job of representing the American people, or do they do such a poor job that a third major party is needed?

Americans' Opinion of the Two-Party System								
	Oct 2003	Sept 2006	Sept 2008	Sept 2011	Oct 2013	Sept 2015	Sept 2017	Jan 2021
RESPONSE								
Third party needed	40%	58%	47%	55%	60%	60%	61%	62%
Parties do adequate job	56%	33%	47%	38%	26%	38%	34%	33%

Data from: Gallup, Inc.

Americans' Opinion of the Two-Party System, By Party Affiliation							
	Oct 2003*	Sept 2007	Aug 2010	Sept 2012	Sept 2016	Sept 2018	Jan 2021
PARTY							
Democrats	38%	53%	45%	40%	43%	54%	46%
Independents	56%	72%	74%	58%	73%	72%	70%
Republicans	22%	40%	47%	36%	51%	38%	63%

Data from: Gallup, Inc.; *Percentages reflect respondents who stated a third party is needed

1. Do you think the results of these question depend on the party in power at the time the poll was taken?

2. What might be the cause of the up-and-down nature of the views of Americans on the two major parties?

PRIMARY SOURCE

Speech: Concession Speech, Al Gore, December 13, 2000

The presidential election of 2000 between Vice President Al Gore and Texas Governor George W. Bush was one of the closest in U.S. history. A key role in determining its outcome was played by Florida, as its tallies were so close that, by law, a machine recount was required. It resulted in Bush leading by less than 400 votes. Gore demanded a hand recount, which led to legal proceedings on its constitutionality. The case of *Bush* v. *Gore* quickly reached the U.S. Supreme Court, where the manual recounts were ruled a violation of the 14th Amendment's Equal Protection Clause. After a tense and uncertain time, the outcome was decided, and Gore conceded the election to Bush.

Neither he [President-elect Bush] nor I anticipated this long and difficult road. Certainly neither of us wanted it to happen. Yet it came, and now it has ended, resolved, as it must be resolved, through the honored institutions of our democracy. . . .

Now the U.S. Supreme Court has spoken. Let there be no doubt, while I strongly disagree with the court's decision, I accept it. I accept the finality of this outcome which will be ratified next Monday in the Electoral College. And tonight, for the sake of our unity of the people and the strength of our democracy, I offer my concession.

I also accept my responsibility, which I will discharge unconditionally, to honor the new president-elect and do everything possible to help him bring Americans together in fulfillment of the great vision that our Declaration of Independence defines and that our Constitution affirms and defends. . . .

Other disputes have dragged on for weeks before reaching resolution. And each time, both the victor and the vanquished have accepted the result peacefully and in the spirit of reconciliation. . . .

And while there will be time enough to debate our continuing differences, now is the time to recognize that that which unites us is greater than that which divides us.

While we yet hold and do not yield our opposing beliefs, there is a higher duty than the one we owe to political party. This is America and we put country before party. We will stand together behind our new president.

1. What is the central idea expressed in Gore's concession speech?

2. Why do you think it was important for Gore to concede the election following the decision in *Bush* v. *Gore*?

PRIMARY SOURCE

Political Cartoons: The Electoral College, 2004, and The U.S. Election Without the Electoral College, 2016

Almost without fail in recent years before and after each presidential election, the benefits and drawbacks of the Electoral College are debated by political analysts as well as regular Americans. Does it work? Is it fair? Should it be replaced? The debate continues to this day.

This cartoon by Mike Keefe, a Pulitzer Prize-winning cartoonist, was drawn following the 2004 presidential election during which a State constitutional amendment was on the ballot in Colorado that would change the way their Electoral College assignments would be made from winner-take-all to proportional. The amendment failed to pass.

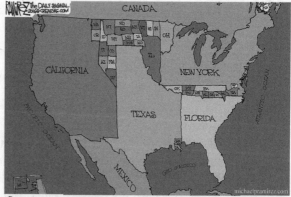

This cartoon by Mike Ramirez, a two-time Pulitzer Prize-winning cartoonist, was drawn following the 2016 presidential election and parodies the size of each State according to the size of each State's population and the influence it would have if the election of the President were to be by popular vote.

1. What does Keefe suggest about the Electoral College through the way in which he depicts it in his cartoon?

2. In the cartoon by Ramirez, is he trying to communicate support for or opposition to replacing the Electoral College? How do you know?

3. Do you think the opinion illustrated in Keefe's cartoon is still widely held in the debate over the Electoral College today? Why or why not?

Lesson 1 Types of Economic Systems

CLOSE READING

Capitalism and the Factors of Production

1. **Draw Inferences** Could any individual take a series of courses on entrepreneurship and become successful? Why or why not?

The American Free Enterprise System

2. **Explain an Argument** The text states that politics and economics are inseparable. Explain why this is true in a free enterprise system.

3. **Analyze Interactions** Although a capitalist system is said to have four fundamental factors, one of those factors—individual initiative—could be viewed as an essential element of the other three factors. Explain this integrated way of looking at the factors.

What Is a Mixed Economy?

4. **Draw Conclusions** In the United States, why might certain businesses find it in their best interest to operate in one State as opposed to another?

Socialism, Communism, and Karl Marx

5. Cause and Effect Consider the ideals behind socialism. Describe the climate that might exist in a country that is ripe for accepting a socialist approach.

Communism

6. Summarize To explain why Mikhail Gorbachev insisted on both openness and restructuring, summarize what the situation in the Soviet Union had become as a result of communism.

The Special Case of China

7. Determine Central Ideas When countries such as China emerge from communism, they often require foreign investments. Why?

Comparing the Free Enterprise System with Other Economic Systems

8. Compare and Contrast At which points on the scale shown below do the following labels belong? Answer by writing each label in the box below its number on the scale: (A) Laissez-Faire, (B) Communism, (C) Mixed Economy, (D) Socialism.

Levels of Regulation

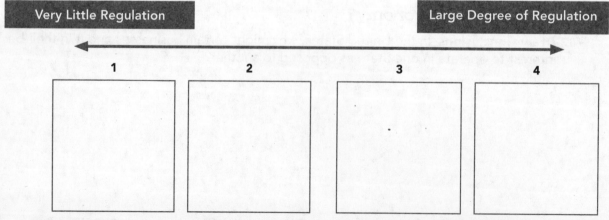

Lesson 2 Fiscal and Monetary Policy

CLOSE READING

The Federal Government and the Domestic Economy

1. **Determine Central Ideas** Summarize the role of the Federal Government in the American economy.

2. **Summarize** Describe how three different governmental institutions carry out the role of the Federal Government in the domestic economy.

Key Goals for the Economy

3. **Draw Conclusions** What is the gross domestic product (GDP), and what usually happens when the GDP increases at a steady rate?

4. **Identify Supporting Details** What is the Consumer Price Index (CPI), and why is the Bureau of Labor Statistics in charge of reporting it?

How Fiscal Policy Influences the Economy

5. **Identify Supporting Details** As you read "How Fiscal Policy Influences the Economy," use this graphic organizer to record details of how fiscal policy can be used for the two following purposes: (1) to control economic growth and (2) to slow inflation.

To Grow Economy	To Slow Inflation

6. **Cite Evidence** In the midst of the Great Depression of the 1930s, British Economist John Maynard Keynes advocated a two-pronged approach to dealing with the economic disaster. What did Keynes's approach call for the government to do?

How Monetary Policy Influences the Economy

7. **Summarize** What tools are available to the Federal Reserve Board (the Fed) to influence the nation's economy?

8. **Explain an Argument** Which of the tools that is available to the Fed to influence monetary policy might produce the quickest results? Why?

Lesson 3 Financing Government

CLOSE READING

The Power to Tax

1. **Determine Central Ideas** Why is the power to tax so important that the Constitution lists it first among the powers of Congress?

2. **Identify Cause and Effect** How does the tax rate paid by individuals affect the nation's economy?

3. **Analyze Interactions** How does collecting taxes from businesses affect the nation's economy?

4. **Draw Inferences** Why is it important that the Federal Government not be able to tax State governments in the exercise of their proper governmental functions?

Federal Taxes Today

5. Categorize Why can payroll taxes be considered a form of social welfare?

6. Evaluate Explanations How does the power to tax affect the business community?

7. Analyze Interactions How do regressive and progressive taxes affect people of different economic classes?

8. Evaluate Explanations Does it work for government to try to discourage certain behaviors, such as smoking or drinking alcohol, by imposing a "sin tax"? Why or why not?

Lesson 4 Spending and Borrowing

CLOSE READING

Federal Expenditures

1. **Compare and Contrast** What is the difference between controllable and uncontrollable spending?

2. **Identify Supporting Details** As you read "Federal Expenditures," record notes in this graphic organizer about the top four federal spending priorities.

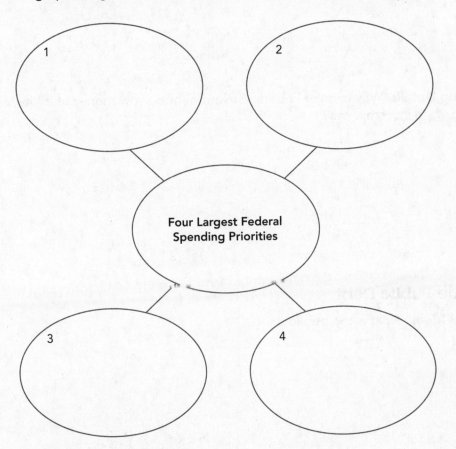

Creating the Budget

3. **Identify Key Steps in a Process** What is the President's role in the budget-making process?

4. **Identify Key Steps in a Process** What is Congress's role in the budget-making process?

Borrowing and the Deficit

5. **Identify Cause and Effect** How does the Federal Government borrow money? Does anyone benefit from this borrowing system, or is anyone disadvantaged by it?

6. **Identify Supporting Details** Why can the Federal Government borrow money at a lower interest rate than private investors can?

Understanding the Public Debt

7. **Determine Central Ideas** What is the public debt?

8. **Draw Conclusions** Is concern over the size of the public debt justified? Why or why not?

Lesson 5 The U.S. in a Global Economy

CLOSE READING

A Global Economy

1. **Determine Central Ideas** What are the advantages for the United States to trade with other countries?

2. **Analyze Interactions** How can you predict a country's most likely trading partners? Include the United States as an example in your answer.

U.S. Trade Policies

3. **Compare and Contrast** Compare and contrast tariffs and import quotas using the Venn diagram below. Consider the advantages and disadvantages of each for the United States.

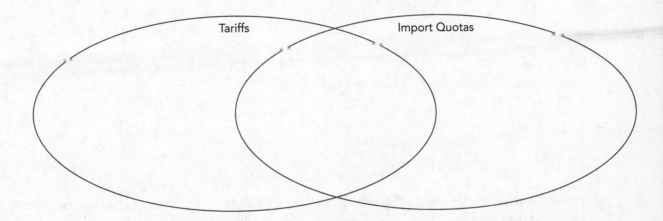

Tariffs   Import Quotas

4. **Explain an Argument** What arguments are made by those who support NAFTA (the North American Free Trade Agreement)? What arguments are made by those who oppose it?

Trade Alliances and Organizations

5. **Summarize** What is the purpose of trade organizations, such as the WTO (World Trade Organization) and the Group of 7?

6. **Analyze Interactions** Why do countries need regional trade alliances as well as global ones?

The Consequences of the Global Economy

7. **Identify Cause and Effect** What is a trade deficit, and how does a trade deficit affect the United States?

8. **Draw Conclusions** How has the role of the United States in the international marketplace changed over time?

PRIMARY SOURCES

Speeches: Two Views on the Federal Budget

The annual federal budget represents many competing interests. To what programs and agencies should the money received from taxpayers, corporations, and other sources be given? This is the vital question that must be answered during the budgeting process in Congress each year.

Ideally, the money coming in is enough to cover all expenses; even more ideal is having funds left over after the bills are paid. But in all the years since 1789, this country has rarely been in that situation. Instead, the government often borrows money to meet its expenses. Economists as well as politicians disagree on the impact of federal debt on the nation's economy.

Senator Mike Lee, July 29, 2019

. . . we're talking about paving the way for us to spend a whole lot more money through the federal government than we would otherwise spend, this is occurring at a time when Americans are already required to work many weeks, in some cases many months out of every year just to pay their federal taxes.

In addition to this, after that, they're told, by the way, that's not enough. It's not nearly enough. Because for a long time, the federal government has been spending a lot more money than it takes in.

. . . [W]e've got a government that's too big and too expensive. . . .

Young Americans, . . . [are] going to be responsible for [a $22 trillion debt]. Notwithstanding the fact that all of that debt has been accumulated at periods in their life either before they were born or before they were old enough to vote. This amounts to in a sense, Mr. President, a really pernicious [devious] form of taxation without representation. . . .

. . . there are those in Congress who will maintain that we shouldn't worry about discretionary spending, . . . because . . . the bigger threat is in fact about mandatory spending.

It's the entitlement programs they will say is driving the debt crisis. But it's important to point out, Mr. President, we're not reforming those either.

Now look, I know I will be the first to admit there are no easy solutions here. . . .

Is it going to be any easier [later] to deal with the [deficit] problem than it is now? I think not. If not us, who? If not now, when?

"Reexamining the Economic Costs of Debt," Chairman John Yarmuth, House Committee on the Budget Hearing, November 15, 2019

. . . Traditional economic theory has long warned that persistent budget deficits and rising government debt would increase interest rates and discourage private-sector investment, curbing economic growth over the long run. But over the last several decades, interest rates have instead steadily declined to record lows even as the debt has soared to near-record highs. Today, . . . the United States pays a significantly lower interest rate on a 10-year loan than it did 20 years ago. . . .

A more . . . realistic view of the costs of debt makes it clear that our fiscal policy should be driven by our nation's needs rather than an excessive and inflexible focus on debt. Accordingly, the most urgent priority facing policymakers today is addressing deficits in the real economy, rather than in the budget. Failing to tackle severe and persistent infrastructure, education, and health outcome deficits is arguably more damaging to our economic and fiscal outlooks than the risks posed today by higher debt. . . .

Deficits that support critical investments in families, communities, and environmental resilience—investments that improve current and future living standards and boost our long-term growth potential—are justified uses. So are fighting recessions and avoiding needless and destructive austerity [government policies to control public debt] traps.

---

1. Why does Senator Lee feel that deficit spending is the same as "taxation without representation"?

2. According to Chairman Yarmuth, how can large deficits be justified?

Supreme Court Case:
National Federation of Independent Business v. Sebelius, 2012

In March 2010, the Affordable Care Act (ACA) was signed into law by President Barack Obama. Its main goals were to make health insurance affordable and available to more people, to expand Medicaid to cover more low-income adults, and to lower healthcare costs overall. Controversial from the start, the new law was taken to court almost immediately by a number of States.

In late 2011, the Supreme Court agreed to consider the rulings of several cases combined under *National Federation of Independent Business* v. *Sebelius.* Among the points considered was the constitutionality of the individual mandate, which required Americans to purchase a minimum amount of health insurance or be financially penalized.

Majority Opinion, Chief Justice John Roberts

Under the mandate, if an individual does not maintain health insurance, the only consequence is that he must make an additional payment to the IRS when he pays his taxes. That, according to the Government, means the mandate can be regarded as establishing a condition—not owning health insurance—that triggers a tax—the required payment to the IRS. Under that theory, the mandate is not a legal command to buy insurance. Rather, it makes going without insurance just another thing the Government taxes. . . .

. . . Congress's authority under the taxing power is limited to requiring an individual to pay money into the Federal Treasury, no more. If a tax is properly paid, the Government has no power to compel or punish individuals subject to it. We do not make light of the severe burden that taxation . . . can impose. But imposition of a tax nonetheless leaves an individual with a lawful choice to do or not do a certain act, so long as he is willing to pay a tax levied on that choice. . . .

The individual mandate cannot be upheld as an exercise of Congress's power under the Commerce Clause. . . . [H]owever, it is reasonable to construe what Congress has done as increasing taxes on those who have a certain amount of income, but choose to go without health insurance. Such legislation is within Congress's power to tax.

1. What options do citizens have regarding the individual mandate according to the Court's assertion of its constitutionality?

2. Which words or phrases used by Roberts suggest that the Court was interpreting the law's intent?

Lesson 1 State Constitutions

CLOSE READING

The First State Constitutions

1. **Compare and Contrast** After reading "The First State Constitutions," compare and contrast the United States Constitution and State constitutions.

2. **Use Visual Information** Look at the image of the Massachusetts constitutional convention. Discuss the impact of this event on how State constitutions are drafted and approved.

State Constitutions Today

3. **Identify Supporting Details** As you read "State Constitutions Today," use this concept web to record the six categories of State constitutions. Include a brief note about each category.

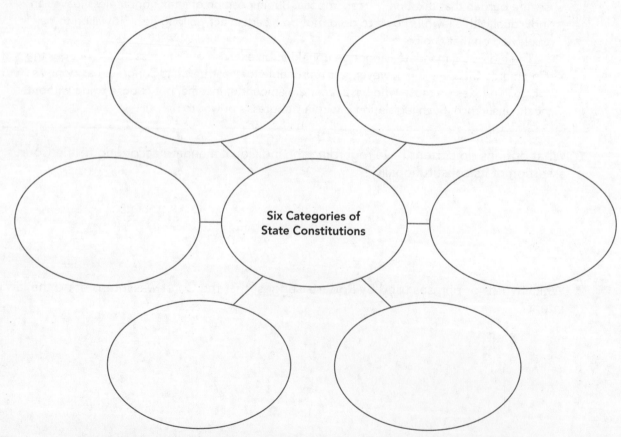

Six Categories of
State Constitutions

4. **Infer** Why do you think most States cover the subject of governmental structure in very specific detail in their State constitutions?

Constitutional Change

5. **Identify Steps in a Process** Using the information in this Topic, and the "How to Propose Changes to a State Constitution" chart, describe the major steps in the process of changing a State constitution.

The Need for Reform

6. **Summarize** What are the two main problems highlighted in the text regarding State constitutions and their need for reform?

7. **Draw Inferences** Why do you think that many State constitutions remain so lengthy and unnecessarily detailed and have so many outdated provisions?

Lesson 2 State Legislatures

CLOSE READING

The Legislature

1. **Compare and Contrast** As you read "The Legislature," "State Legislators," and "Powers of the Legislature," use this graphic organizer to record the main facts about State legislatures. Use the information you compile to answer this question: What are the similarities and differences of State legislatures?

Structure	Powers	Organization

State Legislators

2. **Hypothesize** What are the advantages and disadvantages of the high turnover rate in legislative seats?

3. **Support a Point of View with Evidence** How might State legislatures that meet on a part-time basis be more representative of the people than those meeting full time?

4. **Analyze Information** Consider the "Supreme Court Decisions" timeline as you answer the following question: What Court decision was *most likely* used to decide the 2012 redistricting dispute, in which minority groups accused the Texas State legislature of drawing maps that discriminated against them?

Powers of the Legislature

5. **Make Generalizations** What is the *police power*? In what ways does a State's police power serve to ensure the health and welfare of the State's citizens?

6. **Contrast** How do the States' legislative and nonlegislative powers differ in addressing the needs of citizens?

Organization of the Legislature

7. **Cite evidence** Support this statement using evidence from the text: " . . . presiding officers regularly use this power (to appoint the chair and other members of each house committee) . . . to . . . work their influence on the legislature and its product."

Direct Legislation

8. **Support Ideas with Evidence** Do you think that initiatives and referenda are effective ways for voters to influence or control government? Explain your thinking with evidence from the text.

Lesson 3 The Governor and State Administration

CLOSE READING

The Governorship

1. **Identify Patterns** The governor of a State shares power with the lieutenant governor and other executive officers. Fill in the chart to identify the powers of individual executive officeholders in a State, and show which powers apply to the executive, judicial, or legislative branches of government.

Responsibility	Officeholder	Branch of Government
commands State militia		
interprets State laws		
records official State proclamations		
presides in senate		
pays State bills		
pardons convicted criminals		

2. **Identify Cause and Effect** Would limiting the number of times a governor may be reelected in your State also limit the power of the governor? Explain your answer.

3. **Identify Cause and Effect** How does the formal policy for removing a State governor from office protect both the citizens and the governor?

The Governor's Powers

4. **Compare and Contrast** Which is limited more by a State constitution—the governor's legislative powers or appointment and removal powers? Explain your answer.

5. **Identify Steps in a Process** List legislative and judicial steps that a governor could take to help pass a law restricting the use of the death penalty.

Other Executive Officers

6. **Interpret** How does government power become limited when one person fills the dual roles of lieutenant governor and president of the senate?

7. **Analyze Charts** Look at the "Choosing Executive Officers" chart. In your opinion, which system of selecting and filling executive officers—federal or State—creates the most effective government? Explain what makes it "effective."

Lesson 4 State Courts

CLOSE READING

State Courts and the Law

1. Draw Conclusions Why do you think common law remains important to our legal system?

2. Use Visual Information Look at the flowchart titled "The Use of Precedent." What is the significance of the arrows pointing downward from the middle row of cases to the ruling?

Understanding the Jury System

3. Identify Supporting Details As you read "Understanding the Jury System," use this graphic organizer to record details of the two basic types of juries in the American legal system.

Types of Juries	
Grand Jury	Petit Jury

4. **Draw Inferences** Most government processes in this country must take place in public, but a grand jury does its work in secret. Why do you think this is?

How the State Courts Are Organized

5. **Summarize** Describe the work of the general trial courts.

6. **Vocabulary: Use Context Clues** Why are magistrates called the "city cousins" of justices of the peace?

How Judges Are Selected

7. **Explain an Argument** How do you think judges should be selected? Choose one method described in this text, and create a strong, well-supported argument for that method.

8. **Identify Supporting Details** What qualifications do you think a good judge should have? Write a help-wanted advertisement for your ideal candidate.

Lesson 5 Local Governments

CLOSE READING

Counties Across the United States

1. **Summarize** Many counties are governed by a group often called the *county board*. Summarize the structure and role of the county board. Use examples from the text to support your answer.

Tribal Governments

2. **Draw Conclusions** What are the advantages for Native American tribal governments of a government-to-government relationship with the Federal Government?

Towns, Townships, and Special Districts

3. **Determine Meaning of Words** The term *town meeting* is used in the text to describe local government in New England. Define the term *town meeting*, using details from the text to enhance your definition.

4. **Cite Evidence** Explain why township borders have been drawn differently in different States and at different times, citing historical evidence from the text.

City Government

5. Explain What impact has the population shift from rural to urban areas had on local governments? Draw from the text to support your inference.

Forms of City Government

6. Summarize Cities across the United States use several forms of government. Drawing from the text, summarize the most important aspects of those forms of government in a table-style graphic organizer.

Most Common Forms of City Government		
Characteristics of Each Form		

City Planning and Other Municipal Functions

7. Identify Supporting Details What details under "City Planning and Other Municipal Functions" support the idea that most American cities developed "haphazardly," with "no eye to the future"?

Suburbs and Metropolitan Areas

8. Cite Evidence Explain the consequences of "suburbanitis," citing evidence from the text.

Lesson 6 State and Local Spending and Revenue

CLOSE READING

Education, Public Health, and Welfare

1. **Integrate Information** Use the graphic organizer below to record information about State services and sources of revenue as you read the text. Then refer to your completed graphic organizer as you answer the question that follows.

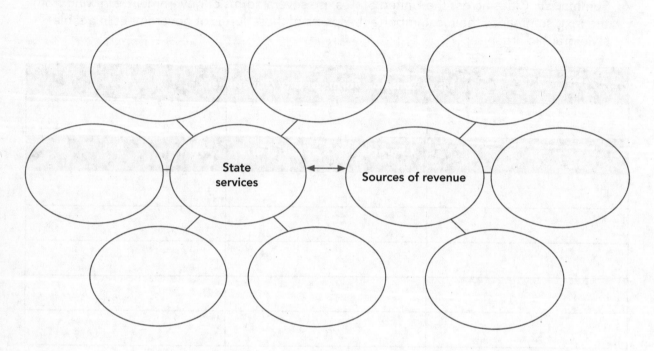

What is the major challenge faced by the States as they work to serve their citizens?

2. **Cite Evidence** Refer to the text as well as the graphic titled "Education Spending Per Student," covering actual and projected per-pupil education expenses, to cite evidence supporting the following conclusion: The education of State residents is one of the most important responsibilities of every State.

Public Safety, Highways, and Other Services

3. Make Generalizations Why are public safety and highways services best provided by State governments rather than the Federal Government? How do States interpret this responsibility? Use specific information from the text to support your answer.

Financing State and Local Government

4. Hypothesize Review Adam Smith's third principle of a sound tax system from his book *The Wealth of Nations*. Why do you think it is important that paying taxes be convenient? Is this principle met with the State sales tax?

> "Every tax ought to be levied at the time, or in the manner, in which it is most likely to be convenient for the contributor to pay it."

Sources of State Revenue

5. Generate Explanations Explain the difference between a sales tax and an income tax. What are the advantages and disadvantages of each in terms of equality and equity among constituents?

6. Make Inferences What is the goal behind the imposition of a selective sales tax?

State Budgets

7. Generate Explanations How does the executive budget process used by most States provide a form of checks and balances between the executive and legislative branches?

PRIMARY SOURCE

Supreme Court Case:
Cooper v. *Aaron*, 1958

On February 20, 1958, five months after the school integration crisis involving the Little Rock Nine (a group of nine Black students who enrolled at the formerly all-white Central High School in Little Rock, Arkansas), members of the school board, along with the Superintendent of Schools, filed a suit in a U.S. district court calling for the suspension, or temporary halt, of the school's desegregation plan. The court granted this request, an act that openly resisted the Supreme Court's decision in *Brown* v. *Board of Education*, which claimed that racial segregation in public schools violated the 14th Amendment. However, the U.S. Court of Appeals for the Eighth Circuit reversed the lower court's ruling, and the case made its way to the Supreme Court. In this landmark case, the Court ruled unanimously that the halting of the school's desegregation plan directly resisted the federal mandate for desegregation and that State governments and legislatures are in fact bound by federal court orders.

Per Curiam [Unanimous] Opinion by all Members of the 1958 Warren Court

As this case reaches us, it raises questions of the highest importance to the maintenance of our federal system of government. It necessarily involves a claim by the Governor and Legislature of a State that there is no duty on state officials to obey federal court orders resting on this Court's considered interpretation of the United States Constitution. Specifically, it involves actions by the Governor and Legislature of Arkansas upon the premise that they are not bound by our holding in *Brown* v. *Board of Education*. . . .

It is, of course, quite true that the responsibility for public education is primarily the concern of the States, but it is equally true that such responsibilities, like all other state activity, must be exercised consistently with federal constitutional requirements as they apply to state action. The Constitution created a government dedicated to equal justice under law. . . . The principles announced in that [*Brown* v. *Board*] decision and the obedience of the States to them, according to the command of the Constitution, are indispensable for the protection of the freedoms guaranteed by our fundamental charter for all of us. Our constitutional ideal of equal justice under law is thus made a living truth.

1. What limitation does this Court decision put on States' rights, particularly regarding education?

2. How does this text classify State authority over public education?

Speech: State of the State Address, Florida State Governor Ron DeSantis, March 5, 2019

The State of the State Address is an annual speech delivered by the governors of every State in the nation. Much like the annual State of the Union Address delivered by the President, this speech typically reflects on the current conditions of the State and outlines the governor's plans for new State policies and legislation. The governor will usually emphasize the role the State government plays in the fields of education, public welfare, public safety, and transportation.

Mr. President, Mr. Speaker, members of the House and Senate, Cabinet members and Supreme Court Justices: Mindful of the economic opportunities that lie before us, understanding the environmental challenges that require our attention, and conscious of our obligations to education and public safety, I consider myself blessed to stand before you, at this particular moment in our history, as Florida's 46th governor. . . . and I'm optimistic that this legislative session provides us with a unique opportunity to advance needed reforms in a variety of different areas that will strengthen our state and benefit the people now and in the future . . .

I observed during my inaugural address that, in the words of Alexander Hamilton, energy in the executive is the leading character in the definition of good government. . . .

. . . Executive energy and leadership are necessary to meet fully the challenges that are before us—but they are not sufficient. In a constitutional system with separated powers, we—the political branches—must work together so we can build off the foundation that has been laid and set the stage for the future success of our State.

How can we accomplish this task? I answer simply: be bold—be bold in championing economic opportunity, be bold in protecting Florida's environment, be bold in improving education, be bold in defending the safety of our communities, be bold because while perfection is not attainable, if we aim high we can achieve excellence.

1. What topics does Governor DeSantis choose to highlight in this speech? Why might this be?

2. Why might Governor DeSantis, a State official, choose to include a quote from Alexander Hamilton, a fervent supporter of a strong National Government?

PRIMARY SOURCE

Political Cartoon: Self-Serve Road Repair, Ed Fischer, 2009

Among the numerous responsibilities of State governments is the building, operation, and maintenance of roads and highways. Drivable roads, of course, are crucial for citizens, whether it be for their morning commutes or weekly trips to the grocery store. However, when roads are in disrepair, they can be obvious signs of the shortcomings of State governments.

1. What is the main criticism about State governments that the cartoonist is trying to communicate?

2. What does this cartoon imply about State government spending?

Lesson 1 Democracy and the Changing World

CLOSE READING

Transitions to Democracy

1. **Draw Inferences** Explain why the role of reformers is important in a dictatorship.

2. **Draw Conclusions** Why is democratization such a vital step in a country's transition to democracy?

Examples of Transitions to Democracy

3. **Use Visual Information** Refer to the text and the timeline "Germany's Path to Democracy." What are some factors that had to develop for East Germany and West Germany to successfully reunite?

4. **Determine Central Ideas** Explain why Mikhail Gorbachev is considered a reformer instead of a hard-liner. Then describe how he helped the Soviet Union to change.

Outcomes of Transitions to Democracy

5. **Identify Key Steps in a Process** How might the United States help other countries build strong, independent democratic institutions?

6. **Use Visual Information** Refer to "What Makes Democracy Succeed?" Which of the factors listed do you think is the most important for a democratic system of government to take root and flourish? Explain your response.

Democratic Change and Continuity Today

7. **Draw Inferences** Consider the Middle East and Egypt's struggles as they transition to new governments. How can religious and linguistic divisions pose challenges for a government in transition?

Lesson 2 The United Kingdom

CLOSE READING

A Legacy of Constitutionalism

1. **Compare and Contrast** How did democracy come about in the United States compared to the United Kingdom?

2. **Use Visual Information** Look at the map of the United Kingdom in the text. Describe the country's primary geographical feature, and explain how it has affected the formation of the United Kingdom's government.

Government in the United Kingdom

3. **Identify Supporting Details** Describe the features of the United Kingdom's Parliament.

4. **Determine Central Ideas** How does a coalition work in the United Kingdom's government, and why is it necessary?

5. Summarize Complete the graphic organizer to show how the government of the United Kingdom is chosen and organized.

Official Institution	How Chosen?	What Role or Powers Does This Person/Group Have?
Prime Minister		
House of Commons		
House of Lords		
Cabinet		
Monarchy		

Public Policy and Elections

6. Compare and Contrast According to the text, the winning party in Parliament creates and carries out policy with overwhelming party loyalty based on the party's platform. How is this similar to and different from the United States Congress?

7. Identify Cause and Effect In the United States, elections tend to be candidate centered, while in the United Kingdom, elections are party based. How does the structure of each government play a role in how elections are carried out?

Comparison to the United States

8. Categorize What is the difference between a federal system of government and a unitary system of government? Use examples from the reading to support your answer.

Lesson 3 The Russian Federation

CLOSE READING

Russia and Its History

1. **Summarize** Describe the actions of Vladimir Lenin and Joseph Stalin and their impact on the government of Russia.

2. **Draw Conclusions** What were the most significant events that contributed to the formation of the Russian Federation and its transition to a democratic republic?

3. **Identify Supporting Details** What details under "Reform Led by Gorbachev" support the idea that the transition to a democratic Russian Federation was not easy?

Government in the Russian Federation

4. **Identify Supporting Details** Describe the elements of the Russian executive branch that contribute to the nature of government in the Russian Federation.

5. **Compare and Contrast** How are the offices of the United States Vice President and the Russian Federation prime minister alike? How are they different? Use information from the text to support your answer.

6. **Use Visual Information** Look at the "Organization of Russian Federation Government" chart in the text. Write a description of the Federal Assembly, comparing it to the United States Congress.

Public Policy Creation

7. **Use Visual Information** Look at the image of the Udmurtneft oil field. Explain the significance of this image and the impact of this and similar scenarios on the presidency of Vladimir Putin.

Comparison to the United States

8. **Compare and Contrast** As you read "Comparison to the United States," use this graphic organizer to compare and contrast the governments of the United States and the Russian Federation.

Comparison of Two Governments

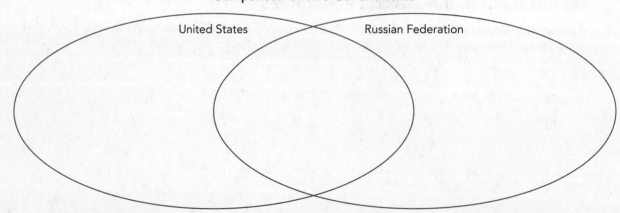

United States   Russian Federation

Lesson 4 China

CLOSE READING

China and Its History

1. **Draw Inferences** Under Mao Zedong's leadership, teachers and intellectuals were bullied, and artists and scholars were sent away to farms. Why was this done, and how did it help Mao pursue his Cultural Revolution?

2. **Draw Conclusions** What did Deng Xiaoping and his government demonstrate to the Chinese people at Tiananmen Square?

Government in China

3. **Determine Central Ideas** The Communist Party has 82 million members, which only translates to about 6 percent of the Chinese public. How is the Communist Party still in power?

4. **Analyze Interactions** Why is the United States in the awkward position of being officially pro-Taiwan but also recognizing the status of the People's Republic of China?

Comparison to the United States

5. **Compare and Contrast** Complete the first two columns of the chart to show how the role of the media has been the same and different in China under Mao Zedong and today. Then, add information from the text and your own general knowledge to show the role the media plays in the United States.

Role of Media during Cultural Revolution	Role of Media in China Today	Role of Media in U.S. Today

PRIMARY SOURCE

Speech: Lecture on Public Issues, Óscar Arias Sánchez, President of Costa Rica, September 21, 1987

Costa Rica is one of the oldest and most successful democracies in Central America. In the late 1980s, however, it was surrounded by nations that were rife with political unrest. During his first term as president of Costa Rica, Óscar Arias Sánchez developed and promoted a peace plan that he believed would resolve the turmoil in Central America. He received the Nobel Peace Prize in 1987 and a number of other accolades for his work.

Development and peace are inseparable. Underdevelopment and widespread poverty breed violence. Nothing undermines the struggle for development more than a threat to peace. The internal peace and external security of any nation depend upon that nation's capacity to produce and to distribute the basic needs of its citizens. . . .

We believe that domestic tranquility and external security may be attained in our hemisphere only if freedom and democracy prevail in all of the countries. There can be no peace while the press is censored, while freedom of thought is stifled, while opposition groups are persecuted, while the pulpit is silenced, while the ballot box is violated, and while society is subjected to the arrogance of the bayonet. Because of these aberrations [misconducts], dictatorships are obstacles to peace. We must promote change within those regimes. . . .

. . . For the Latin American people, the most desired goal is that democracy may spread and thrive. We have paid dearly for authoritarian regimes—politically, socially, and economically. The fall of each despot has left in its wake suffering, torture, forced exile, and other abuses that have scarred deeply the face of the hemisphere. . . .

When I assumed the office of president of Costa Rica, I spoke of the necessity to create an alliance to support freedom and democracy in the Americas. A democratic government is the only road to lead us out of poverty, dependence, and war. There should be no place in our hemisphere for tyranny because tyrants threaten peace and violate human rights. . . .

. . . We must make peace and put an end to the hatred that reflects many decades of poverty and desperation. We must construct a new economy, without delay. Without economic growth we will not be able to attain social justice that millions of Central Americans desperately demand.

1. According to Sánchez, what are the two most important factors to achieving peace in Central America?

2. How difficult do you think it would be to "promote change" within an authoritarian regime? How could change be achieved?

Document: Joint Statement of Media Freedom Coalition on Media Freedom in Russia, October 28, 2021

After the fall of the Soviet Union, Russia adopted a new constitution. It included a guarantee of freedom of the press and forbid censorship. It did not take long, however, for those freedoms to disappear. Accusations of Russia's suppression of the press arose quickly, but Russia continuously denied any wrongdoing. In recent years, Russia's treatment of journalists has again become very harsh. In 2021, in response to an increase in the mistreatment of journalists, a joint statement was signed by 19 nations, including the United States, demanding that Russia stop its politically motivated repression of the press.

This year has seen the Russian authorities systematically detain journalists and subject them to harsh treatment while they reported on protests in support of imprisoned opposition figure Aleksey Navalny [leader of the Russia of the Future political party]. In April, the office of student journal DOXA was searched in relation to spurious [phony] charges and four editors were then subjected to severe restrictions on their freedom. On June 29, Russian authorities raided the apartments of staff members of investigative news website Proekt on the same day the outlet published an investigation into alleged corrupt practices by Russia's Interior Minister. Proekt was added to Russia's list of "undesirable foreign organizations," the first media entity to receive that designation. In addition, Russian occupation authorities in Crimea have held Radio Free Europe/Radio Liberty (RFE/RL) reporter Vladislav Yesypenko since March and have reportedly tortured him in detention. On July 15, Yesypenko was indicted on specious [deceptive] charges and faces up to 18 years' imprisonment. . . .

In an unambiguous [unmistakable] effort to suppress Russians' access to independent reporting, the Russian government introduced onerous [burdensome] labeling requirements for so-called "media foreign agents" last year. Since then, it has charged RFE/RL with more than 600 violations, resulting in fines totaling more than $4.4 million. . . . It increasingly appears the Russian government intends to force RFE/RL to end its decades-long presence in Russia, just as it has already forced the closure of several other independent media outlets in recent years.

1. In today's world, do you think it is possible that the Russian authorities could successfully repress the voices of independent journalists in Russia? Why or why not?

2. What is the long-term impact of people in Russia not having easy access to uncensored journalism?

PRIMARY SOURCE

Document: Chapter I: General Principles, Constitution of the People's Republic of China, 2018

The People's Republic of China has had four constitutions since the republic was established in 1949. Although it has been amended several times over the years, the constitution of 1982 remains the nation's "law of the land." The U.S. Constitution and China's constitution both describe the structure and powers of the government; however, that is where the similarities end. As a socialist state, the People's Republic included very different details in its constitution, as illustrated by the excerpt below from the General Principles portion of China's constitution.

> **Article 1** The People's Republic of China is a socialist state governed by a people's democratic dictatorship that is led by the working class and based on an alliance of workers and peasants.
>
> The socialist system is the fundamental system of the People's Republic of China. Leadership by the Communist Party of China is the defining feature of socialism with Chinese characteristics. It is prohibited for any organization or individual to damage the socialist system. . . .
>
> **Article 6** The foundation of the socialist economic system of the People's Republic of China is socialist public ownership of the means of production, that is, ownership by the whole people and collective ownership by the working people. The system of socialist public ownership has eradicated the system of exploitation of man by man. . . .
>
> **Article 9** All mineral resources, waters, forests, mountains, grasslands, unreclaimed land, mudflats and other natural resources are owned by the state, that is, by the whole people, except for the forests, mountains, grasslands, unreclaimed land and mudflats that are owned by collectives as prescribed by law. . . .
>
> **Article 24** . . . The state shall champion core socialist values; advocate the civic virtues of love for the motherland, for the people, for work, for science and for socialism; educate the people in patriotism and collectivism, in internationalism and communism, and in dialectical and historical materialism [a philosophical world view] and combat capitalist, feudal and other forms of decadent [unwholesome] thought. . . .
>
> **Article 28** The state shall maintain public order, suppress treason and other criminal activities that jeopardize national security, punish criminal activities, including those that endanger public security or harm the socialist economy, and punish and reform criminals.

1. How would you describe the tone of the language used in this document? Is it similar or different from that used in the U.S. Constitution?

2. Which articles do you think could be used as justification for the suppression of political dissent? Why?

Photography

Topic 6
72: Sidney Harris/CartoonStock

Topic 9
109: Mike Turner/CartoonStock

Topic 10
127: Tribune Content Agency, LLC

Topic 11
138L: Mike Keefe/Intoon.com; **138R:** By permission of Michael P. Ramirez and Creators Syndicate, Inc.

Topic 13
166: Ed Fischer/CartoonStock

Text Acknowledgements

Topic 1
From President Barack Obama's Inaugural Address, January 2013.; "The Spirit of Liberty," Learned Hand, speech presented in Central Park during "I Am an American Day," May 21, 1944; From Majority Opinion, Justice William R. Day, Buchanan v. Warley, U.S. Supreme Court, November 5, 1917

Topic 2
From Nigerian Constitution of 1999; Preamble to the United States Constitution; Majority Opinion Sutherland, United States v. Curtiss-Wright Export Corp, ET AL.; Journal of William Maclay

Topic 3
Excerpted from "For the Equal Rights Amendment," Representative Shirley Chisholm, Speech to the House of Representatives, August 10, 1970; From "What's Wrong with 'Equal Rights' for Women?," by Phyllis Schlafly, The Phyllis Schlafly Report, February 1972; Letter to Congress Supporting Puerto Rico Statehood Admission Act, from 51 Puerto Rican organizations, March 2021

Topic 4
Majority Opinion, Justice O'Connor, appeal to Shaw ET AL. v. Reno, Attorney General, ET AL., U.S. Supreme Court; Speech of Joseph McCarthy, Wheeling, West Virginia, 1950; From Declaration of Conscience, Margaret Chase Smith, to Congress June 1950.

Topic 5
From The Land of Hope: An Invitation to the Great American Story by Wilfred M. McClay, 2019. Published by permission of Encounter Books, c/o Writers' Representatives LLC, New York NY 10011, www.writersreps.com/permissions. All rights reserved.; Majority Opinion, Justice John Paul Stevens of Clinton, President of the United States v. City of New York, U.S. Supreme Court, 2000

Topic 6
Press Briefing by Ari Fleischer, White House, September 12, 2001; Report on the UN Charter, Senator Tom Connally, Congressional Quarterly (Senate), June 28, 1945

Topic 7
From In Conversation with U.S. Supreme Court Justice Sonya Sotomayor, February 14, 2019, Library of Congress.; Majority Opinion, Justice Byron White, United States Supreme Court TAYLOR v. LOUISIANA,1975.; Presidential Radio Talk: Supreme Court Justices, Ronald Reagan, August 9, 1986

Topic 8
From On the Duty of Civil Disobedience by Henry David Thoreau, 1849.; Lemon v. Kurtzman, 1971, Majority Opinion, Warren E. Burger, U.S. Supreme Court; Lemon v. Kurtzman, 1971, Dissenting Opinion, Bryon White, U.S. Supreme Court

Topic 9
Majority Opinion, Justice Samuel Alito, Supreme Court case Ledbetter v. Goodyear Tire & Rubber Co., Inc; "I, Too" by Langston Hughes, Weary Blues

Topic 10
From John F. Kennedy, Address "The President and the Press" Before the American Newspaper Publishers Association, New York City.; Majority Opinion, Justice Samuel Alito, US Supreme Court Brnovich, Attorney General of Arizona, ET AL. v. Democratic National Committee ET AL.

Topic 11
Popular and applied graphic art print filing series/ Library of Congress Prints and Photographs Division Washington, D.C.[LC-DIG-ppmsca-59409]; From Al Gore's Concession Speech, December 13, 2000

ACKNOWLEDGMENTS

Topic 12

From speech by Senator Mike Lee to U.S. House Budget Committee, July 29, 2019; From Hearing: Reexamining the Economic Costs of Debt by the U.S. House Budget Committee, November 2019.; From Justice John Roberts, Opinion of the Court, June 28, 2012, National Federation of Independent Business v. Sebelius, Secretary of Health and Human Services, U.S. Supreme Court

Topic 13

U.S. Supreme Court Opinions: Cooper v. Aaron, 358 U.S. 1,1958.; Governor DeSantis' State of the State Address, March 5, 2019

Topic 14

From Lecture on Public Issues, Óscar Arias Sánchez, President of Costa Rica, September 21, 1987; Joint Statement on Media Freedom Coalition on Media Freedom in Russia, Media Note, Office of the Spokesperson US State Department, October 28, 2021; From Chapter I: General Principles, Constitution of the People's Republic of China, 2018